EMPOWER

EMPOWER

The Leg to ... volunteer Movement

JEFF MARTIN

EMPOWER

The 4 Keys to Leading a Volunteer Movement

JEFF MARTIN

B&H
PUBLISHING
NASHVILLE, TENNESSEE

To Julie, you will always have my heart.
Without your encouragement, this book
would have never gotten outside of my thoughts.

AJ, Ashleigh, and Alexis,
you make me the most blessed dad on earth.

Mom and Dad, your Godly example has provided
a light unto my path. Thank you.

Acknowledgments

I would like to thank all the volunteers I have had the privilege to work with over the last thirty years. The patience and trust you extended to me has been astounding. Thank you for locking arms in causes both great and small. You are difference-makers!

Special thanks to two of those volunteers who were the first to hear about the idea for Fields of Faith and immediately responded with one question, "What do you need?" Thank you, Chuck Abshere and Dan Horton. You would be two of the faces I would sculpt into the Mt. Rushmore of volunteers.

To the B&H gang, thank you to my editor, Taylor Combs, for coaching me up in my writing and giving me the words of encouragement I needed during the process. I appreciate Jenaye White for casting out the book to as many people as possible. Thanks to Josh Green for getting the ball rolling.

Thanks Dan Deeble of Lost Ball Consulting for helping me craft complex ideas into a clear, compelling message. Your encouragement and coaching were timely and inspiring. You quickly compared me to a mad scientist. You get me.

The Fellowship of Christian Athletes has always been volunteer intensive and I have been honored to serve on the staff. John Odell believed in me to let me pursue a lot of ideas that were outside of the box, always providing support and guidance to keep me and my crazy ideas in line. Thanks to Dan Britton for his innate ability to see what works and make it work better. He immediately saw the potential of Fields of Faith and served as a catalyst for it to spread across the country.

Finally, I wish to recognize my family. First to my wife who has been my teammate on the front lines. She has given up a lot for our relentless pursuit of God and the ministry he has assigned for us in so many places. She's my best friend and my true love.

To my kids, AJ, Ashleigh, and Alexis. You are evidence of God's grace that he would allow me to be your father. I'm thankful to have two more members of the family with Sydney and Colby choosing to hitch their wagon to our family.

To Jerry and Bernie, you raised an incredible daughter and allowed me to marry her. That was a true leap of faith! Thanks for being unwavering fans and supporters of our family.

Thanks to my brother-in-law, Jeff Madison, for the countless hours we have spent discussing and comparing ministry and military strategy around the world over many decades. To my sisters Becky and Kathy who have allowed me to antagonize them from an early age until today with a great sense of humor and unwavering bond that only siblings can experience.

To Jack and Sharon Martin, my parents who have walked with me through my life journey. I love you and thank you for your tireless prayers and support through this roller coaster called life. You are a rock, a north star that lights the way in the dark. You don't just talk about the way of Jesus, you follow it.

Contents

Preface

Movements that unify millions of people around a common cause and have ongoing national impact over the course of two decades are rare. They're also incredibly hard to plan and predict. This is especially true if the core of the movement is based on volunteers as the primary pillars on which everything stands.

Add to that scenario minimal funding, no centralized infrastructure, no facilities, no marketing or advertising department, no social media teams or technology department support, and the birthing of that movement appears laughable if not impossible.

But that is exactly what we saw happen . . .

I was inspired in 2002 to start pursuing a vision of gathering students, churches, businesses, and entire communities at their local athletic field on one night. I called it "Fields of Faith." The goal was for students to be the primary speakers and for the message to be the same at every event. The message would be a personal challenge from the students to engage the Bible on a daily basis and come to faith in Christ. Giving students the microphone in that setting was countercultural, but it was the main part of the program.

God did something astounding. The first year we had seventeen participating stadiums, small and large, in three states. Our motto was "One Day. One Message. One Stand." More than six thousand people attended, and many lives were changed. In the following decade the movement continued to spread to the point that currently more than five hundred stadiums and a quarter of a million people gather together every year to hear the students share in their communities.

Over the course of sixteen years, more than two million people have been impacted by Fields of Faith, and that number continues to grow each year.

This book is not about Fields of Faith. It is about the four keys of starting and growing a movement—principles I discovered from Fields of Faith. These four keys are value, simplicity, commonality, and ownership. My desire is not to provide statistical analysis, expert consultation, or a reproducible template on how to start and expand a movement in your organization or business. All I know is what I saw. This book is my attempt to peel back the layers and take people on a journey of what happened, which may help spark other movements in a new way.

Welcome to the journey.

PART 1

CONNECTING THE DOTS

CHAPTER 1

UNTAPPED
POTENTIAL

Ordinary

> When they saw the courage of Peter and John
> and realized that they were unschooled, ordi-
> nary men, they were astonished, and they took
> note that these men had been with Jesus. (Acts
> 4:13 NIV)

Everyone has a deep desire to make a difference with their
lives. They want to be part of something bigger than themselves.

Many people volunteer with organizations in an attempt
to satisfy this desire. They get involved only to be relegated
or relegate themselves to being spectators. They believe real
impact and power are reserved for the elite, gifted leaders, with

celebrity-like status, who have been put on a pedestal of influence seemingly unreachable to the ordinary person.

These involved spectators believe they could never be like those celebrities. They are ordinary, yet each volunteer senses that inside of them resides something epic. The truth is that every volunteer is sitting on a powder keg of influence, but they just don't know how to ignite it.

> Every volunteer is sitting on a powder keg of influence, but they just don't know how to ignite it.

A recent *Forbes* online article by Mallory (Blumer) Walsh titled "The Real Problem with Influencer Marketing: You're Focusing on the Wrong 'Influencers'" reveals how this truth is being realized in the hyper-competitive world of business marketing, causing a massive strategic shift in long-established tactics: "Only 23% of people believe content from celebrities and influencers is influential. Alternatively, 60% say content from friends or family influences their purchasing decisions."[1]

The business world understands the rising influence that ordinary people have on the product decisions of their peers, and they are adapting their strategies with lightning speed to seize this opportunity. Can the same be said of the ministry

---

[1] Mallory (Blumer) Walsh, "The Real Problem with Influencer Marketing: You're Focusing on the Wrong 'Influencers,'" *Forbes*, October 5, 2018, accessed February 8, 2020, https://www.forbes.com/sites/forbescommunicationscouncil/2018/10/05/the-real-problem-with-influencer-marketing-youre-focusing-on-the-wrong-influencers/#26ca760a42d7.

world when it comes to their message of abundant and eternal life through Jesus Christ?

In a rapidly deteriorating modern culture, ministries are starting to scrutinize their strategies and tactics in a desperate attempt to curb the tide of secularism engulfing everything in its path. In this pivotal moment there has been a gradual awakening of untapped power that can change a culture—the untrained, ordinary volunteer.

There are millions of them, and they sense they are being overrun and overlooked in every aspect of their lives.

What would it look like if volunteers realized the power of the "untrained, ordinary," collectively owning and celebrating their influence in a great movement of God? Is this what Satan fears most and has hidden best?

I recently heard a pastor put it this way when speaking at a youth leader conference about ordinary students: "Students today have the passion. They are simply waiting for permission to pursue a mission!"

God has always used the ordinary to stun the world. He hasn't changed. He's simply waiting for us, His ordinary people, to step into the influence each of us already has and win our world for Christ.

This is not mere theory or ancient history. I have had a front-row seat to watch it happen in our time since I started Fields of Faith.

Clean the Trucks

"Can I have your blessing to ask your daughter to marry me?" I nervously asked Julie's father. I had practiced this question in my head many times, and I actually delivered it with only a slight crack in my voice.

"Yes, you can," he responded. "On one condition. You must have a job before you do it."

I had just been accepted into Southwestern Baptist Theological Seminary in Fort Worth, Texas, and was planning to move there from Oklahoma City. I hadn't had a chance to finalize all the details about the move, but I now had a razor-sharp focus on my first priority: *get a job as fast as possible.*

This was before the time of scouring the Internet for job postings. I had to physically make the four-hour drive to the campus. A job postings board in the administration building had a few cards pinned to the board which featured a "help wanted" section. As I scanned through the various cards, one of them jumped out as something I could do that would fit my class and study schedule.

The seminary had a facilities maintenance department that was responsible for all the maintenance and operations necessary to support the large campus. The department employed many of the students who came to the seminary from a variety of trade professions, which allowed them to go to seminary and work for the school using their skill sets as plumbers, electricians, auto mechanics, and many more.

The Physical Plant Facility was advertising positions for those professional trade skills of which I had none. There was one part-time position, however, that I might possibly qualify for despite my limited work experience and zero technical skills. The position called for someone who could take care of the fleet of work trucks used by the professionals during the day. The trucks needed to be washed, cleaned, and fueled at the end of each day.

I copied down the address and drove the short distance to the physical plant located on the edge of the seminary property. The auto shop section featured four work bays equipped with enough lifts and tools to keep the fleet of fifteen to twenty work trucks, as well as every other construction vehicle up and running around the clock.

After I had a short interview with the automotive repair department boss, he surprisingly offered me the job on the spot. I still remember how I felt walking away from that building after securing that part-time job. I didn't care what the job was. All I knew was that I had met the requirements set by the father of the woman I wanted to marry. I wasn't walking on concrete as I left; I was walking on clouds!

When fall arrived, I had moved into the dormitory and begun my four-year pursuit of a master of divinity degree. It was invigorating. Our wedding date was set for the following summer in May. I rolled up my sleeves and went to work. I would attend classes during the day and work in the evenings. All the students who worked for the physical plant and possessed a professional, technical skill set would go to class during the day and put in their work hours around their class schedule until 5:00 p.m. Once the day was over, they would return their work trucks to the physical plant and drive home to their families and evening studies.

I would pass the students leaving the plant as I drove in to work at 5:00 p.m. I would then work hard until 9:00 p.m. each evening. I would follow that up with a one-hour workout at the gym, then head to my dorm room to study. The physical plant had a truck wash bay as well as its own gas pumps. I would run each of the trucks that had been used that day through the wash bay, using the high-pressure wand to clean off all the dirt that had accumulated on the vehicles that day. Next, it was time to throw away any trash in the vehicles, which usually included some fast-food bags, cups, and wrappers. I would then use a rag and Armor All to wipe down and protect all of the inside surfaces. To finish up, I would shine the tires and fill the gas tank before returning the now-glistening trucks to their preassigned parking spot ready for use the next morning.

This routine went on for the entire scholastic year. I didn't think anything of it. It was providing me with some needed income, but most importantly, it was one of the main reasons for the upcoming wedding. I was as happy as a pig in mud.

Eventually the wedding day came, followed by a romantic honeymoon with my beautiful bride. Then it was time to return to my work and study routine.

During my first year of seminary, I began to look for a church that might need an aspiring minister with zero experience but ready and willing to serve. It seemed like all the seminary students were serving in some capacity in churches in and around the Dallas-Fort Worth area. Many of the students worked part-time for rural churches that dotted the Texas and Oklahoma countryside hundreds of miles away. The churches would often provide a parsonage for the seminary students serving as pastors, youth pastors, education directors, children's coordinators, and worship leaders. They would stay and faithfully serve on the weekends before heading back to school for studies during the week.

I thought that with all the churches in North Texas, I could surely find some position that would allow me to serve, get some much-needed experience, and make a little stipend on the side (which I desperately needed). Besides, I started to notice everyone sharing their weekend ministry stories on Monday mornings. Lives were being changed for Jesus Christ every weekend. Marriages were being saved, youth were making professions of faith, revivals were being held, worship leaders were taking people to the throne of God, the sick and dying were being visited and prayed for by the church. God was on the move!

But I wasn't there to see it. I had no ministry stories. It became harder and harder to hear about what God was doing through everyone around me. I felt like God had purposely put me on the sidelines and wouldn't let me into the game.

Being a lifelong competitive athlete, this did not set well with me. It was like choosing kickball teams at recess in grade school. Two captains—normally the bigger, faster, stronger kids—make alternating picks from the pool of their classmates who want to play. The number of prospective players dwindles quickly until only a few to choose from remain. The worst is to be chosen last. That kid feels of little value, and no kid wants that. This was how I was beginning to feel.

Maybe God didn't see value in me. The other students actually were more talented and gifted in their ability to lead, speak, connect, and serve. Had I made a wrong choice to go to seminary? Had I really heard the call of God on my life into ministry? Doubt started to creep into my head and heart. In no time the creep broke out into a full-on sprint.

In my current mental condition, I was not prepared for what God was about to reveal to me.

It was another sweltering Texas day in August. I remember seeing the heat waves rising off the blistering asphalt as I drove to work each afternoon. You could crack an egg on concrete and serve it over easy in moments. It was absolutely miserable.

When I first started my job a year earlier, I arrived ready to do it with excellence. My blue industrial work shirt with my name stitched into the white label above the left pocket would be crisp and clean. I always had it tucked in so I wouldn't appear sloppy. I had a pep in my step and a readiness to work hard, just like my dad had taught me and modeled with his own actions my whole life.

With each passing day that I couldn't find a ministry position like everyone else, my gratefulness and desire to work hard at my job began to wane. I gave myself a new job title: truck janitor. Dragging myself to work became increasingly difficult. At the end of the evening, my clothes would be saturated with sweat. The heat had a way of sucking out a little bit of your soul with each passing hour. I got to the point where I didn't care if my shirt was tucked in or if I looked sharp. I still got my job done every day, but I was the only one there in the evenings, so why should I care how I looked?

My talks with God began to change. All I had anymore were questions. *Why wouldn't He put me in the game? Had I done something wrong? What was His plan for me? Why had He placed me on the corner of a dusty shelf, hidden away from all the action?*

I felt surrounded by an army of gifted and talented ministers of the gospel actively making a massive difference in the world, and then there was me, the sweaty, blue-collar, truck janitor "changing the world" one clean truck at a time.

That soon changed.

It was another sweltering Texas day in August. I had dragged myself to the physical plant for another round of work. I looked nothing like a motivated employee. I was moping around. My jeans were dirty; my wrinkled shirt was untucked and smelled of yesterday's sweat. My face looked ragged and worn out.

As I got out of my car, I walked over to a cinder-block wall, climbed on top of it, and just looked at the sky. I had been reading about David in the Old Testament. I just finished the classic story of David and Goliath. I had read the story many times, always focusing on the great combat scene and how David showed incredible courage, overcoming all odds and rallying all the men to unite in an overwhelming defeat of the Philistines. But a slight nuance in the story had emerged for me. The narrative leading up to the great battle caught my attention.

With the powerful Philistine army threatening the people of Israel, a call went out for all the young warriors of Israel to rise up and meet them in battle. An old man named Jesse, from Bethlehem in Judah, had eight sons. The three eldest joined the army of Israel. David was the youngest. While everyone around him was out fighting a great battle for Yahweh, David, the youngest of the brothers, was given the exciting job of herding sheep.

But he also had a part-time gig as basically an Uber Eats driver delivering food for his brothers on the front line. He was then told to return to his isolated job of caring for his father's herd of sheep. He did it faithfully, making sure they had green pastures in which to feed, clean water from bubbling streams in the hills, and protection as they slept at night against predators like lions and bears.

As I was sitting on that wall and pondering the story of David, a realization slowly descended on me. I had been sitting with my back to the truck parking lot. (I literally had a hard time looking at the trucks when I arrived each evening.) I turned my sweaty head around and stared at the trucks. David had been given an assignment from God that was different from all the others who were fighting battles in the army of God. His main assignment was to take care of sheep far away from the fight. The sheep had white wool and black hooves. As I gazed intently at the trucks sitting motionless in the parking lot, a burst of clarity overcame me. I clearly saw a group of all white trucks that had all black tires, the same color scheme as a herd of sheep.

This was a watershed moment for me. It was as if I suddenly woke up, rubbed my eyes, and saw my surroundings clearly. This wasn't just about a menial job cleaning a group of trucks. This was my herd of sheep that God had assigned to me! I needed to clean them, feed them gasoline, and put them to bed in the evening before locking up the complex to protect them from being vandalized or taken in the night.

I remember tears forming in my eyes as I realized how I had become so disenchanted and ungrateful with God's assignment for me. He was shaping me into what He wanted me to be in His timing. I had been continually comparing myself with everyone out there on the front lines of ministry, which had led me to a severe lack of value in myself as well as the assignment God had given to me.

My immediate response was to ask God to forgive me for being so selfish. My next response was to tuck my shirt in. This was a simple move, but it was symbolic for me, similar to rolling up your sleeves to get to work. I only had short sleeves, so tucking my shirt in was the next best thing.

The change in perspective immediately affected everything for me inside and out. Outwardly, my clothes, posture, facial expression, and pace changed. Inwardly, my joy, confidence, thankfulness, anticipation, and faith were all buoyed in an instant when I saw those trucks through a heavenly lens. They were my herd of sheep, and that was good enough, which meant I was good enough. A sense of freedom and calm descended on me.

I remember attacking my job that evening with a new zeal fueled by appreciation. This was my opportunity to express my thankfulness to the Lord by doing my job with excellence. Those trucks didn't belong to the seminary; they belonged to God— no different from the small herd of sheep assigned to David thousands of years earlier.

My problem was that I had been focusing on my conditions instead of my convictions. If I truly believed God valued me and had an assignment for me each day, my only option would be joy in what He had given me and entrusted to me to do each

day. Whether it was winning souls or washing trucks, the
conditions made no difference. Only faithfulness mattered.

> **Whether it was
> winning souls or
> washing trucks, the
> conditions made
> no difference.
> Only faithfulness
> mattered.**

That intersection with God
on that hot Texas afternoon
changed me. I've needed to be
continually reminded of that
truth time and time again, but
God has always been patient
and persistent with me. He
valued me, and this awareness
inspired me to give my best and
own the part He had given me.
This lesson would serve me well in the years to come, allowing
me to see opportunities I otherwise would have missed.

RECAP

Great influence resides in the untrained, ordinary volunteer.
This must be realized before it can be revealed.

Our conditions often blind us to the conviction that we each
have great value. When we remember this, it changes our out-
look, affects our actions, and impacts those around us regardless
of the conditions.

CHAPTER 2

FOR KING AND CULTURE

Josiah

Every now and then, there are moments in our lives when time stands still. This was one of those moments for me.

Our house was situated in the prairie of southwest Oklahoma in a small town called Cache, just south of the Wichita mountain range.

The Wichita Mountains jut up out of the mixed-prairie grassland with a rocky, rugged landscape featuring large boulders, cedar trees, creeks, lakes, and a mountain peak called Mount Scott that ascends out of the prairie. The region has been home to a rich variety of wildlife including elk, white-tailed deer, pronghorn antelope, mountain lions, gray wolves, black bears, prairie dogs, and massive herds of bison.

Not only is the location spectacular, but the history is as well. Due to the ongoing Indian Wars in the region during the 1800s, the U.S. Army established Fort Sill as a strategic site to engage the Indian tribes. The infamous General George Armstrong Custer was involved in selecting the site in 1868. The great Comanche chief Quanah Parker had resided in Cache, Oklahoma, and the feared Apache chief Geronimo was detained at Fort Sill, where he eventually died as a prisoner of war.

In 1901, President Theodore Roosevelt, an avid big game hunter who had participated in several hunts in the region, issued a proclamation creating the Wichita Forest and Game Preserve as the nation's first big-game animal refuge.

I was sitting on my back porch enjoying a hot cup of coffee, preparing to spend my daily time of reading God's Word. I was staring out over our property that contained several buffalo wallows, large circular indentions in the prairie made over the centuries by buffalo rolling in the water after a rain, creating permanent shallow watering holes. Meadowlarks were singing as a gentle wind swept through the swaying tall grass.

Sitting in this pristine setting, I should have been inspired, but I was deeply disturbed.

My oldest son AJ was getting ready to cross into a key milestone of every kid's life. He was on the verge of becoming a teenager. I had two daughters right behind him, Ashleigh and Alexis. Like any parents, my wife, Julie, and I loved them more than we did our lives, and we wanted to protect and provide them with everything they would need to succeed in life.

Julie and I had been clearly called into ministry and had answered the call from the beginning of our marriage. After serving together as interns at a church in Arkansas, we got engaged and I was accepted to Southwestern Seminary. When we got married, we moved into our first home in seminary housing, where we lived until I completed my master of divinity degree with biblical languages three years later. Upon graduation, I accepted a position as the senior high youth pastor at a large church in Del City, Oklahoma, serving under a dynamic pastor, Tom Elliff, who would soon become president of the Southern Baptist Convention. We threw ourselves into our work and were part of God doing some incredible things during our four-and-a-half-year tenure at the church.

We learned so much during our time there, but God had a new assignment for us in the southwest corner of the state as an area representative with the Fellowship of Christian Athletes. FCA was started in Oklahoma in 1954. Since that time, it has been challenging coaches and athletes on the professional, college, high school, junior high, and youth levels to use the powerful platform of sport to reach every coach and every athlete with the transforming power of Jesus Christ.

After all those years, staff offices had been established to minister to coaches and athletes in every part of the state except southwest Oklahoma. That was about to change.

I was approached to consider starting an office in Lawton, Oklahoma. I had come from a long line of athletes and a strong Christian upbringing. My wife had become a Christian as a result of a high school coach giving her a Bible and helping her understand what it means to have a personal relationship with Jesus Christ.

Due to these connections with FCA, the offer moved our hearts. After Julie and I prayed about it, we realized this was God's plan for our lives and uprooted our growing family to move to Lawton.

For the next eight years, we put our hand to the plow. God always provided. We were amazed to see how God moved through the coaches, athletes, churches, and volunteers in southwest Oklahoma. Lives were changed and restored as only God can do. We were simply along for the ride.

But on this morning I found myself staring with tired eyes toward the western horizon. Something had not been sitting well inside of me for the past several months.

I had slowly been coming to grips with a chilling fact. For more than a decade I had given my life to doing everything I could to take the gospel to a desperately lost world. I wanted to change the culture for Christ. My particular focus had been where all spiritual awakenings tend to occur—*teenagers*.

We had hosted cutting-edge events. Trained key leaders. Spoken at what seemed like endless events. Rallied countless volunteers. Discipled many coaches and athletes. And now my own children were getting ready to walk into that teenage cauldron, and a chilling fact suddenly hit me like a Mack Truck.

In previous generations, it seemed to be more of a balanced fight for parents to protect their children from the negative aspects of the world. Straight, linear battle lines were drawn up with the families, the church, and other institutions of good on one side and secular belief systems, organizations, and godless initiatives on the other side. The forces of good were able to hold the lines and many times push back against the forces of evil.

But something happened. The battle lines were redrawn. The forces of good began to show cracks in the line. Little by little, the forces of evil exploited those cracks. Soon they had penetrated the lines and poured through with stunning speed.

It was no longer a linear battle. It was now asymmetrical warfare, a 360-degree, 24-7 fight.

The secular culture now had access to my children from countless angles. What was formerly three channels on TV was now hundreds. What started out as a house phone used to communicate to another person was now a mobile access portal to limitless belief systems, images, music, and ideas in direct, mocking opposition to God. When parents and churches would try to stop the dumping of this trash into their homes by shutting down those who made the trash, they were told it was their individual responsibility to keep it out. The production of trash didn't seem to be affected by political activism; it was protected and accelerated. Even if the trash was eliminated in their home through constant diligence and understanding of the myriad of ways billion-dollar companies were developing to get access to their kids, the parents had no control over the homes of their children's friends. Many of those homes had already been ravaged and destroyed by the world. We were constantly on defense to protect our families, and there was no end in sight to the offensive juggernaut being thrown at us from every angle in this new 360-degree fight.

Having grown up in a family of athletes and coaches that went back several generations, I knew one thing for sure. If your team is in a highly competitive game and you are always on defense, you are not going to win.

The culture my children were walking into had not moved closer to God over the past two decades. It had actually moved further away from God and with breakneck speed. The followers of Christ were not taking ground; we weren't even holding ground. We were *losing* ground.

I was sitting in a haze of disillusionment. It seemed like we had tried everything, and we were making absolutely no difference to turn the tide. I felt like I had been throwing deck chairs off the *Titanic* in a feeble attempt to keep it from sinking.

> If your team is in a highly competitive game and you are always on defense, you are not going to win.

What else was there?

The only thing I knew to do was reluctantly open the Bible that was sitting in my lap for my daily reading. I did this every morning to start out the day. It seemed so simple, but it was all I had at that moment.

I was in the process of reading through the entire Bible over the course of a year. The passage for that day was in the Old Testament book of 2 Chronicles 34. I needed some inspiration at that point, and I couldn't recall a lot of inspirational quotes from 2 Chronicles floating around. But I went ahead and started reading since it was the next chapter up.

It started with a story about an eight-year-old king named Josiah. At the age of sixteen he began to seek the God of David in a time of almost universal godlessness and corruption. The succession of two wicked kings, Manasseh and Amon, Josiah's father and grandfather, had stripped away any and all evidence of the Hebrew God who had miraculously saved His people from slavery in Egypt through Moses, led them into the Promised Land through Joshua, and established a powerful dynasty through David and Solomon. Gone were the stories of mighty faith, victory against all odds, and humble obedience to the one true God. These were distant memories, fables of a forgotten era. The new normal was marked by deep heathenism that appeared to have been structured around taking everything the book of the law recorded about God's instructions on how to live and doing the opposite.

One of the main directives from God to His people was never to worship any other gods besides Him. Yet these kings set up altars to worship the entire host of heaven. The Canaanite gods took precedence and became prominent fixtures in the Judean countryside. Asherah poles were erected along with altars to Baal, considered to be the lord of the gods.

Baal was seen as the god who controlled the heavens, which meant he controlled the rain. This was as important to the agrarian economy of the ancient world as it is today. If there is no rain, there are no crops, and all livestock will die resulting in the starvation and death of all the people. This is why Elijah set up the test with the prophets of Baal to see which god could bring down fire from heaven. It was a test of who controlled the heavens, which was easily won by God in dominating fashion. But the lessons of history tend to fade into fable as new generations seek to make their own mark.

The wicked kings were not content with setting up altars to the Canaanite gods; they took it one step further. They actually had some of these altars built inside the temple of God, which would be the highest form of institutional blasphemy possible in Judah or Israel. Manasseh even descended into the worship of Molech, which demanded child sacrifice. The idol of Molech was a bronze statue with a large bronze bowl at its base. The statue would be heated from a blazing fire pit located directly underneath the statue. When the bronze bowl was white hot, infants would be thrown into the bowl to burn to death. Manasseh even "sacrificed his son in the fire" (2 Kings 21:6) of Molech.

This was the appalling, godless world Josiah was born into—a world that had been totally sanitized of any hint or memory of the God of the Hebrews. The God of Abraham and Isaac had been removed from public view and hidden in the dark recesses of a marginalized, broken-down temple for a forgotten God.

Despite being born into such a dark, hyper-heathen culture, a small light began to flicker in the heart of the eight-year-old king. His biblical résumé is as follows: "He did what was right in the LORD's sight and walked in the ways of his ancestor David; he did not turn aside to the right or the left" (2 Chron. 34:2).

God grabbed his heart, and Josiah chose to leapfrog the sin-stained legacy of several previous generations in his bloodline. Instead of aligning with Manassah and Amon, he chose to align with the warrior-king David.

When he was sixteen, he began to seek the God of his ancestor David. The effort needed to seek what he was looking for was immense. There was nothing available to show Josiah who God was and the path to find Him—just ancient echoes of a once-powerful God who had been removed and replaced with Canaanite idols.

One thing we know about the God of the Hebrews is that when someone, regardless of their age or culture, begins to faithfully seek Him with all their heart, they will find Him. Josiah connected himself to the vine, and fruit began to grow.

At the age of twenty, he began to take action on what was welling up in his heart. He knew that the idols were wrong, and he did something based on common sense. *He removed them!*

In a heathen culture this is considered extreme, intolerant, and radical. In God's economy this is simple obedience. This was Josiah's starting point: simple common sense. No one had taken this first step for several generations. But one step always leads to the next.

When he was twenty-six years old, Josiah began to clean out the temple of God. This next step led to the discovery of an old, dusty scroll. It was the book of the law written by Moses.

As the supervisor of the cleaning crew gave a progress report to Josiah, he mentioned at the end of the report that he had found a book. Josiah's curiosity was piqued, and he asked to see it.

The transfer of that parchment into the waiting hand of Josiah caused a seismic shift in the spiritual, societal, and political trajectory of the entire country of Judah. The Word of God changed everything.

Josiah began to scan the document. It contained instructions and guidelines on how to know and obey the God of his ancestors. The connection was immediate. What Josiah was doing instinctively was now coming into focus with abundant clarity. Each word he read sank deep into his soul. The reality of the depths of sin his country had fallen into sent shivers down his spine—so much so that he tore his clothes in despair. What he had done was not enough. The country had not been doing what God wanted because they didn't know what He wanted them to do. Disaster was coming on Judah, and it was coming with the vengeance of a holy God.

As leaders always do in times of distress, Josiah acted. This problem was one that had infested all of the population from the greatest to the least. The vaccine for this sickness had to be applied to everyone. Josiah instructed his leaders to immediately assemble the entire population at the now-cleansed temple. Once the masses were gathered, he did another simple, commonsense thing. He read aloud to them the book of the law.

In one fell swoop God used Josiah to synchronize the hearts and minds of the people of Judah with His eternal, divine instructions on how they should live.

The Scripture captures this incredible moment in 2 Chronicles 34:31–33:

> Then the king stood at his post and made a covenant in the LORD's presence to follow the LORD and to keep his commands, his decrees, and his statutes with all his heart and with all his soul in order to carry out the words of the covenant written in this book. He had all those in Jerusalem and Benjamin agree to it. So all the inhabitants of Jerusalem carried out the covenant of God, the God of their ancestors. So Josiah removed everything that was detestable from all the lands belonging to the Israelites,

and he required all who were present in Israel to
serve the LORD their God. Throughout his reign
they did not turn aside from the LORD, the God
of their ancestors.

I almost fell out of my chair.

When desperation and solution meet, amazement follows.

What started out as a lethargic, depressing quiet time
with God on my back porch had suddenly transitioned to the
discovery of a potential plan to take the fight to the enemy from
ancient writings that could possibly work in the twenty-first
century.

The similarities between Judah and America were striking.

Judah was a formerly God-honoring culture that had
eliminated God and become exceedingly evil. While Judah
had a covenant with God that the United States has never had,
nonetheless, America was headed from a place of respect for God
to that same godless destination at a rapid rate.

A solution to this dilemma seemed to materialize out of the
fog of disillusionment I was experiencing. It was made up of two
things:

1. A young leader who was searching for God
2. The discovery of the lost Scriptures

It was not a program, a conference, a book, a celebrity pastor, or
a concert. It was simpler than all these.

This had been the lynchpin of change. When it came time
for someone to step up and make a play, Josiah had answered
the call.

A question suddenly formed in my mind: What is the difference between a country that has no Scripture and doesn't read it and a country that has an abundance of Scripture and doesn't read it? The end result is the same, *a godless culture.*

Neither country can know who God really is and how He wants them to live. There are just empty places of worship littering the land with faint echoes of eternity that no one hears anymore.

Could this same strategy work again?

Gather people in the community in one place.

Identify key young people who are diligently seeking God.

Have them share how the Scripture is changing their lives and challenge their peers to join them in reading and following the Word of God.

I couldn't think of any environments at that time where students were given a pivotal opportunity for that to happen. The strategy for decades had been for the youth to gather together in their churches, camps, conferences, and concerts to hear the "experts" (i.e., the adults) tell them about what they had learned from Scripture. If the simple answer for Josiah's time was to reengage God's Word, led by a young person, could that possibly be an answer for us today?

After all, in Galatians the Bible is mentioned as the only offensive weapon in the armor of God. It says it is alive and active, sharper than any two-edged sword. The Scripture says the words recorded on its pages are actually God-breathed. Jesus quoted the Word of God in His epic confrontation with Satan, as if it were a weapon, and He dominated the devil.

I started thinking of the implications if the masses of Christ followers in our time had actually laid down this powerful offensive weapon in favor of only gathering once a week to listen to a few individuals talk about what they knew about God.

If the people of God had willingly laid down their only offensive weapon with which they could drive back the enemy, this meant one thing. We were always on defense and we couldn't win.

This sobering thought lingered in my head and heart. My desire to find out if this was true started me on a journey that would mesh ancient truths into modern culture resulting in a counterintuitive plan to strike back against the world.

RECAP

The spiritual front lines have changed. We are in a 360-degree fight and must go on offense if we hope to win.

Engaging the Bible can change a culture. It doesn't take an expert to start engaging the Scripture and inspire others to do the same.

PART 2

VALUE

"Consider the birds of the sky: They don't sow or reap or gather into barns, yet your heavenly Father feeds them. Aren't you worth more than they?"

JESUS (MATT. 6:26)

CHAPTER 3

RELEASE THE FLOW OF INFLUENCE

The Fair Market of Value

The value you see in yourself as well as those around you can be the difference between maintaining the status quo and inspiring movement that can shake the status quo.

There is a marked difference between value and need. When we value something, we bestow upon it honor, esteem, and worth. When we need something, we are referring to what all people fundamentally require to function in life. Think of the basic physical necessities all humans share like air, water, food, shelter, and safety.

Needs are characterized by their similarities for all people. If needs are not being met, people will cease to function well and will verbalize it through complaints. Value, on the other hand, is highly individualized. It is internal and not as easily detected. Someone can have all of their needs met but feel of little to no value without anyone else even knowing about it.

Organizations, just like people, have fundamental needs. Think of the people, processes, systems, statistics, training, and resources that drive growth and expansion. These needs must be constantly maintained and developed for any organization to drive toward maturity rather than drift to mediocrity or obscurity.

Organizations must be excellent at meeting their needs, or they will cease to function well, and complaints will mount. However, meeting needs can gobble up and demand the focus of individuals and organizations. Groups can become so myopic that seeing opportunities that exist to breathe life and unleash the power that exists within every human can become difficult.

> **It is possible for nonprofits and businesses to see the people connected to their operations as critical to meeting the needs of the organization and yet miss the opportunity to bestow value on those same people.**

It is possible for nonprofits and businesses to see the people connected to their operations as critical to meeting the needs of the organization and yet miss the opportunity to bestow value on those same people. It's not that the people are being mistreated or taken advantage of.

It's just that the process can overlook the untapped potential lying dormant in the hearts of those same workers and volunteers doing their dead-level best to meet the needs of the organization.

Organizations can be lulled into believing that they are functioning at a high level because all of their volunteers or employees are producing, thus meeting the individual and organizational needs. But what if there were a higher level that could be attained by making a few simple adjustments, releasing untapped momentum into what everyone is already doing?

As I walked across the field of twenty-first-century ministry, I slowly began to realize that volunteers inherently had hidden treasure waiting to be unearthed. It was called influence.

One way to release that influence was to place a heightened value on the volunteers. I had always appreciated and celebrated our volunteers. But the nuance of bestowing increased value on them was different and easy to miss.

I began to connect the dots each time I inserted increased value into what we were already trying to accomplish together. I could see the spark in their eyes when it was done right, but it wasn't easy to predict and measure. Nothing that emanates from deep within individual hearts ever is. That is why people and organizations tend to overlook and miss it. But when it is realized, it can inject momentum and movement in small ways that can have a positive impact on individuals and organizations. It can also happen in big ways that can effect change and quickly sweep across an entire culture.

Going Viral

The impact was astounding. More than 500 million global customers in just one year. The incredible speed of expansion was almost unthinkable. The total reach was amazingly diverse including people of every age, ethnicity, and socioeconomic status. The economic impact soared into untold billions of dollars. Communities, towns, and cities were changed overnight. Any business or nonprofit could have only dreamed of having such exponential reach in such a short time.

It was indeed astonishing. The year was 1918. This wasn't some arbitrary business product that became an overnight viral sensation. It was a microscopic virus that attacks the respiratory system called influenza, later to be named the "Spanish flu."

It wasn't just any influenza. This was a pandemic. The global magnitude and spread of the pandemic was accelerated by World War I with masses of troops being transported around the world.

The 1918–19 influenza epidemic infected an estimated 500 million people worldwide—about one-third of the planet's population—and killed an estimated forty to seventy million people with some estimates climbing to 100 million, including 675,000 people in the United States, far exceeding the combat deaths experienced by the U.S. in the two world wars, Korea, and Vietnam combined. It has been described as "the greatest medical holocaust in history."[1]

---

[1] "1918 Pandemic (H1N1 virus)," Centers for Disease Control and Prevention, accessed January 26, 2020, https://www.cdc.gov/flu/pandemic-resources/1918-pandemic-h1n1.html.

The flu virus is incredibly contagious. An infected person need only to cough, sneeze, or talk to release and disperse tiny respiratory droplets into the air. These can be inhaled by people in the immediate vicinity. In addition, if a person touches anything that has the virus on it followed by touching their mouth, eyes, or nose, they will become infected.

Drastic measures were taken by authorities to counter the lightning-fast devastation to their communities. It was difficult to determine what to do since they didn't really know what it was and how it was actively spreading with such speed. There were no effective drugs or vaccines available at the time to treat this new strain of flu.

Two key steps taken to help slow down the unrelenting march of death were distance and cover. Local authorities attempted to establish distance between individuals by banning them from gathering in public places. Theaters, churches, schools, and other closed-in public places were shuttered, in some cases for an entire year, in an attempt to limit the virus from spreading in such tightly packed spaces. Even funerals were limited to fifteen minutes. People were asked to wear fabric masks to cover their mouths when they were in public. In some areas they were denied admittance to streetcars, offices, and other public places without a mask. There was also rising public support to ban spitting, coughing, and sneezing in public.[2]

---

[2] Obviously, at the time you are reading this, another pandemic comes to mind. You can no doubt see the similarities between the 1918 flu and the response to it and the 2020 COVID-19 or Coronavirus pandemic. While it is still too early at the time of this writing to reflect on the outcome or aftermath of COVID-19, its reality will certainly

No central organizational structure or program could lay claim to the recruitment of so many new carriers in such a short amount of time. The people were the structure. Just people going about their daily lives, routines, and responsibilities.

A potent virus only needs to find residence in one person who interacts with other people to impact the world in a short period of time.

When an infected person sneezes or coughs, more than half a million virus particles can be immediately spread to those close by. It doesn't care if it is a popular person, or a talented person, or a wealthy person. In fact, those types of people would hinder the spread of a virus. While many people know about those celebrity types, they don't come into close contact with them. This is critical to a virus spreading quickly. Celebrities tend to be more physically isolated from the public due to their status. Therefore, the ideal scenario for a virus is the masses of ordinary people who are physically interconnected with the people already around them in their daily lives. This creates a superhighway for a highly contagious virus to travel at breakneck speed.

Modern epidemics are terrifying, even with advanced medical technology. But viral pandemics have been around for centuries. The ancients believed a cosmic fluid traveled throughout the heavens and at different times would intersect with the earth. These intersections were invariably bad. They believed this fluid swept through the population from the heavens, totally

_____

strengthen the visual illustration as you're reading about influence. Interestingly, I wrote this section six months before the outbreak of COVID!

disrupting the normal routine of life and causing the death of untold numbers of people.

In an attempt to explain the unseen driving force behind such rapid devastation unleashed on a vulnerable, helpless population, they attributed it to something that could only come from the heavens. They gave these interactions with the cosmos a name. In Latin, it was called *in-fluere*, which meant "to flow."

By the way, this is also the root word for the English word *influence*.

All they knew was what they could see. Where there was a concentration of people, there would appear out of nowhere a devastating burst of death. It appeared to flow into the population unseen and unchecked. It could only come from the heavens. It must be *in-fluere*, the cosmic flow of indirect impact that could not be explained or contained. The only thing they knew was that it was unstoppable.

> The transfer of ideas and beliefs, just like a virus, can happen astonishingly fast when people gather in public places.

When you overlay the spread of a movement with the spread of a virus, you find remarkable similarities. A breakout in both instances depends on vast numbers of ordinary people interacting with other people. The transfer of ideas and beliefs, just like a virus, can happen astonishingly fast when people gather in public places. This is why repressive regimes always seek to isolate movements by shutting down public gatherings and protests. They will seek to do the same in the digital space.

Internet and social media access will be eliminated in an attempt
to keep the virus of beliefs from coming into contact with others.

This truth is imperative for Christians to understand.
Individuals who are considered carriers of the Christian message
are not considered dangerous to society if they stay confined to
their churches and homes. They are not infecting any people
in the public square if they consistently stay with others who
already have their same beliefs. They are effectively contained
and quarantined.

Problems arise for those who wish to stop the spread of
the gospel when the Christian carriers begin to live out and
speak out their viral message beyond the containment of church
buildings and pour out into the public square. This is why
campuses in America are such an access battleground. More
than 99 percent of the population will pass through the portal
of middle school and high school. This concentration of the
population is required to gather in predetermined locations for
a set amount of time. These gatherings are fertile ground for a
pandemic to begin.

This is no different in every business or profession that
contains carriers of the gospel. They simply need to take off their
masks and sneeze or cough Jesus as they go about their daily
lives.

Covering the mouth, on the other hand, will slow down
a virus as well as a movement. If people stop talking about
what they believe, the movement will be effectively stopped. It
is amazing to see how local authorities attempted to stop the
Spanish flu by legislating the control of the mouth with laws
requiring a mask and making it illegal to cough, sneeze, or spit.

Just think of what would happen if modern believers took this truth seriously.

The preeminent principle is that the greatest opportunity for the viral spread of a movement exists when the vast number of ordinary carriers engage those they normally encounter each day as they go about living their lives.

Slow Your Roll

Every organization has a desire for their message or product to *influere*, virally flow into the market. In fact, "going viral" is a modern term used in social media to describe a video or post that is digitally shared across the population at a rapid, unchecked pace. This is what "influence" is all about.

However, the opposite of influence is another Latin term, *involvere*, which means "to roll up" or "to participate." This is the root word for the English word *involve*.

Many times in nonprofit organizations, we ask volunteers to "get involved" in some way, shape, or form in our programs. We are seeking to "roll them up" into our programs and processes to help meet the needs of the organization. This is the direct opposite of *influere*, which seeks to "flow into" the population.

Over the years of my work with volunteers, I began to wrestle with my understanding and approach to leading volunteers. It eventually became evident that this was something I had been missing.

The volunteers I worked with weren't just people to be rolled up and involved in our programs in order to meet our organizational needs. They were people who needed to be released to flow out and influence a dark culture in desperate need of the light found only in Jesus Christ. They were people who collectively influenced untold thousands in their daily lives beyond any program or event I could conjure up.

This slight shift in mind-set had a profound effect on my philosophy of ministry.

I started looking for ways to place more value on our volunteers. I wanted to create more movement, not more management. I wasn't sure exactly how to do that, but I knew it wasn't just throwing a volunteer appreciation party featuring thank-you certificates, a punch bowl, and a sheet cake. If we wanted to unleash influence, we had to adjust our approach.

High Attendance

One of my first encounters with this principle was in my third year as the senior high youth pastor at one of the largest Southern Baptist churches in the country at that time, First Southern Baptist Church of Del City, Oklahoma. Our youth program had students attending our church from thirty-six different schools in the area. Our church was planning for our annual high-attendance Sunday. This consisted of all the various ministry departments planning something special for Sunday school. I had led our youth program with common youth ministry tactics meant to attract youth. I got really good at planning and marketing highly entertaining programs featuring celebrity speakers, worship artists with bright lights and fog machines, pizza, games, and anything else that would get and keep a teenager's limited attention. But I was becoming increasingly disillusioned with this process.

The brighter the light, the bigger the attendance. But there never seemed to be a real spark in the eyes from our forty volunteers that taught our Sunday school classes. They were involved and would dutifully announce and invite their class to attend the show. But what was missing was real ownership of their role. I also noticed that we would have a brief spike in attendance with each event, but our retention rate was abysmal. I felt like our program was operating like a hamster on a wheel, generating lots of activity and energy but going nowhere.

So I decided to try something different this time to get the teachers more engaged in the planning of high-attendance Sunday. I determined to place more responsibility on the Sunday school teachers for getting their class to attend and bring their friends. The plan was to create a university-type class course on high-attendance Sunday. We did a survey of all the students to determine four course subjects. The subjects the students wanted to learn more about were evolution, drugs/violence, sex, and music. We brought in some local volunteer subject matter experts to teach each course—a public school teacher/coach, a policeman, a counselor, and a musician.

No celebrities were invited. There was no curriculum written by some adult expert in another state. Each student would be able to sign up for one of the four subjects until the course was full.

I then engaged my teachers by challenging them to figure out creative ways to get the kids in their class to attend. Their buy-in was critical. My expectation of them was not just to invite their class and hope for the best. This had been the norm, which usually resulted in most of them dutifully filling the need they were asked to meet. This time I challenged them to own whatever way they determined to get their kids there. I told them what their mission was, not how to do it.

Our church had a large staff with multiple ministry departments. When it came time for all the departments to gather for our weekly education staff meeting, we went around the table for each department head to report how they were planning to increase attendance and the budget they needed to make it happen. Each department gave a predictable report featuring special guest speakers, musicians, food, contests, and giveaways. Every one of the plans cost a lot of money with the primary expectation placed on teachers to invite their classes to the department spectator event.

My report was different.

No special anything. No money needed. Just elevate the expectation of the volunteers. When I was done with my report, all I received were blank stares.

"So you're basically doing nothing extra special except having some volunteer presenters and expecting teachers to figure out how to get kids there. That is your plan? It seems a little lazy on your part."

The prevailing expectation of youth pastors at that time was to create amazing spectator experiences that would draw kids to the church and get them involved in the ongoing programs. My plan didn't necessarily fit that mold.

I passed on the sentiments from our education meeting to my teachers the following Sunday. And that is when I saw it. A spark of fire in their eyes.

They realized I was relying on them to own their part for us to succeed. If they didn't come through, our plan would fail. Oh, and I made sure our volunteers knew that most of the leaders didn't think they could do it.

They knew I wasn't being lazy. I simply trusted in them to get the job done. I valued them more than just relegating them to being invitation robots for the umpteenth time.

These small adjustments to our regular strategy unleashed a flurry of innovation and energy from our teachers. One of them planned to host her class for a sleepover at her house including pizza and movies on Saturday night before high-attendance Sunday. That way she knew she could get them to church since they were already at her house on Sunday morning. Another asked to borrow one of the church vans early on Sunday morning to provide a guaranteed ride for their entire class. Another decided to pay for their class of boys to consume an all-you-can-eat breakfast at a local restaurant before church started that morning. Those boys practically begged to get there at all costs that morning! All of them changed up their normal routine. They were not being rolled up; they were freed up to flow into the lives of their students as they saw fit. The tapestry of all this new activity was a thing of beauty.

Our students displayed more boldness about inviting their friends to Sunday school since they knew their friends would identify with what was being taught. After all, they were the ones who had chosen the topics! For the first time I had allowed them to have skin in the game.

When high-attendance Sunday was over, we not only met our goal; we crushed it, and we were the only department to do so. I still remember the high fives and smiles from the teachers and the student leaders. They weren't celebrating a successful spectator program; they were celebrating their united effort that reached more kids, which is the reason they had signed up to volunteer in the first place!

If you want people to own their part, give them a compelling reason to do so.

I took note of the principles I had stumbled upon. The first was this: if you want people to own their part, give them a compelling reason to do so. If that part is always simple and controlled, that is the effort you will get. There is nothing wrong with that. A lot of simple things must be done to keep everything running. You don't want to burn out your volunteers. But, if you change that up at times to include high challenge and freedom to figure out how to make it happen, you will begin to feel the sudden burst of movement like wind hitting the sails of a sailboat. This is what it means to flow into the challenge instead of being rolled up into a process.

The second principle is this: if you want to bestow increased value on volunteers, place heightened responsibility and expectations on them. This can be risky with volunteers. They aren't being paid, which means they can't be required to do something like a paid employee. If they decide not to show up or to do something halfway, you can't fire them. You elevate your risk as a leader, but you also elevate the opportunity for value to be unleashed in ways you've never imagined.

I like to think of elevating responsibility to the point that the overall success or failure of an initiative would rest squarely on their shoulders. In this space volunteers know they are trusted to be more than a cog in a machine.

This is the amazing opportunity organizations have for their volunteers and employees. It is the opportunity to create the conditions for their people to release the hero that lies within each one of them. *Heroes are hard to identify in the morass of the mundane. They always emerge from the fertile ground of adversity.* Something about being a part of a movement that has high expectations with little chance of success straightens the spine and enlarges the heart of every person. A desire deep in the human spirit wants to be part of a high calling, a challenging adventure with an unpredictable outcome against all odds.

Without Maleficent in the form of a dragon, we don't know and don't care about Prince Phillip and true love's kiss. Without Goliath, we never hear about David. Without massive social injustice, no one would have experienced the hero that was Dr. Martin Luther King Jr. Eliminate World War II and Sir Winston Churchill drifts into obscurity.

Heroes are always formed in direct connection with confrontation. Involvement can get people close to confrontation, but influence places them directly on the front lines where they will experience the thrill of victory or the agony of defeat.

We have the opportunity to be a light in the shadows and call out the heroic influence that rests in each one of us. This has never been needed more than at such a time as this.

RECAP

Meeting organizational needs and bestowing individual value are two separate things. Both are important. We must be intentional to create conditions for people involved in our organizations to realize their value.

Influence is about people "flowing into" the public that can result in viral impact. This is about movement. Involvement is about organizations "rolling up" people to participate in their programs. This is about management.

If you want to bestow increased value on volunteers, place heightened responsibility and expectations on them. This will result in people owning their part since there is a compelling reason to own it. If their part is always simple and controlled, then that is the effort you will get.

CHAPTER 4

VALUE YOU

Makeover

Someone mentioned a prayer request in one of the small groups I was in. I've heard lots of prayer requests over the years, but this one was different.

My office was located in Lawton, Oklahoma. The city is home to a United States Army post that serves as home of the U.S. Army Field Artillery School as well as Army Basic Combat Training. It has played a significant role in every major American conflict since 1869.

The prayer request shared was for Sergeant Gene Westbrook. He had been hit by a mortar in combat operations in Baghdad that left him paralyzed from the waist down. The church he was a member of had mobilized to get the word out to pray for Sergeant Westbrook and his family as he was transported back to the States and his new normal. The church community rallied and raised enough support to provide him with a wheelchair-accessible van, giving him the ability to drive a vehicle that would fit him and his family.

We prayed for him and his family and went on with life. Until we heard another prayer request involving the Westbrook family.

One year later the family was driving to visit friends. Gene lost control of the van on the road. It careened off the pavement and slammed into a ditch, causing the van to flip violently. As the dust settled, they realized their nine-year-old son James was injured. Gene wasn't doing well either.

Emergency vehicles arrived and transported Gene and his son James to the hospital. The news coming out of the ER was devastating. James had been severely injured and was now paralyzed from the waist down. Gene had suffered a stroke leaving him with further damage to his right arm and some loss of memory. This new tragedy was almost unthinkable.

The needs of the family were immediately compounded. The heaviness and complexity of the new challenges were overwhelming. Individual churches provided basic needs like meals. Family and friends rushed to be with the family, still in a state of shock. There were so many needs that no one knew where to start. The complexity of needs was staggering the response. The community had good intentions but no organized efforts to maximize their support. Until someone reached out to one of the national TV networks for help. Their plea was heard by the network's hit TV show. Enter *Extreme Home Makeover*.

If you remember the show, you know it would identify families across the country with pressing needs and rush in to meet one of those needs—a new home. The show's producer would identify a local construction contractor who would then coordinate with local companies and volunteers to provide the materials and labor at no charge.

They put out a call to volunteers and businesses in the community to step into the labor and supplies gap for their audacious goal of demolishing the existing house and building an entirely new structure in seven days.

When *Extreme Home Makeover* arrived on the scene, I watched their plan galvanize an entire community into a motivated, organized, and focused unit right in front of my eyes. As each day passed and the structure of the new house began to rise out of the red dirt, the excitement and buzz in the community became palpable.

Local businesses rushed to provide the various building tools and supplies that were needed. People in the community lined up to volunteer their time and talent to fill any position, skilled or unskilled, big or small, to reach the goal. Local restaurants willingly donated food to feed the massive number of volunteers descending on the build site for around-the-clock construction activities. Banks rushed to help organize and provide funds to help in the effort. A local grocery store offered their parking lot to help provide parking space for all of the volunteers. People were needed to help guide the swelling traffic of onlookers that began to bottleneck around the neighborhood where the house was being built. Signs affixed to chain-link fences featuring local businesses that were providing resources for the project began to pop up along the side of the roads surrounding the neighborhood.

Word also got out beyond our small city. The top universities in the state offered the volunteer services of their nationally recognized football teams at the University of Oklahoma and Oklahoma State University. A never-ending stream of media hovered around the neighborhood trying to get an interview with the stars of the show as well as collegiate football stars, local community leaders, and volunteers. Huge spotlights aimed at the construction site filled the night sky as the heavy machinery and skilled craftsman toiled throughout the night to meet the audacious time line looming over them.

The show featured a segment where the family was sent to a site during the week designed to pamper them and provide a brief respite from the challenges they had been facing. When the family returned, they were whisked into a limo and taken to the site of their new home. They exited the limo in front of a large, screaming crowd made up of the volunteers who had just helped build their new house over the past week. However, they couldn't see their new house yet. Their view was blocked by the tour bus used by the stars of the show.

Ty Pennington, the face of the program, did what he always did: he grabbed a bullhorn and passionately thanked all the volunteers. He then asked the family if they wanted to see their new home, and after they excitedly answered yes, he aimed the bullhorn at the driver and, in unison with the crowd, yelled the phrase that became synonymous with the show: "Move that bus!"

The bus slowly pulled away, and the family reacted in shock at a breathtaking new home and perfectly landscaped lawn in place of their former house. The crowd went wild.

Ty then took them on a guided tour of the new home, showing them the unique specs of the house designed specifically for the individual family members.

The show was successful for many years. It was a positive show that featured a real need met by a real solution provided by real people.

I was mesmerized at the stark difference in the community before the TV show entered the picture and after the production crew arrived. Before the show, all of the people and items existed in the community to build the house:

- The volunteers—They already had a desire to help. They were good people. They didn't suddenly become good people when the show arrived in town.
- The businesses and nonprofits—They all possessed the materials and knowledge to build a house in seven days. They were led and staffed with good people who cared about the community.
- The churches—They wanted to help. Many had interceded in prayer and visits to the family. Some of them had already gotten together to organize and meet some immediate, short-term needs.

I learned that one of the key elements that triggered and galvanized the volunteers to achieve an epic goal together was to place high value on them, which sparked a powerful, synchronized movement.

I always wondered if the community would have responded with such interest and excitement if the house were being built by a big construction company and a lot of paid professionals being brought in from the outside. I think people would have been interested because there was a national TV show capturing a story in their city. But it would have only been the interest of a spectator, not the influence of volunteers getting their hands dirty in the attempt to achieve an epic feat together to help one of their own in dire need.

The brilliance of the show was that it didn't just depend on the power of their celebrity hosts. Don't get me wrong: they were incredibly important. But they tied the success or failure of the goal squarely on the volunteers in the community. They extended trust in the community, and the community embraced the risk and the challenge, which forged an unshakable unity and desire to achieve what seemed impossible.

When viewers across the country tuned in to watch the episode, they could identify with the volunteers working feverishly to get the job down. They saw themselves. *Extreme Home Makeover* valued the ordinary with a bold yet simple goal and captured the imagination of the nation in the process.

I remember the pride that existed in our community following the successful completion of the project. Unity in the community was unleashed for a brief, shining moment that engulfed everything in its path.

Value equals power.

Take a Selfie

The principle of value is one that needs to be examined not only by organizations but by individuals as well. There tend to be two types of people when it comes to value—those who overvalue themselves and those who undervalue themselves. In my experience the second type is more prevalent.

However, in a selfie world where many of the younger generation want to be social media "influencers," the center of their world is indicated by the center of their phone camera, which is themselves. This can lead people down a dark path of believing they actually are the center of the world. For most of them, this belief didn't happen in a vacuum. Their parents helped create the environments that allowed it to take root and flourish. An entire generation has been raised with parents who aggressively sought to destroy or disrupt anything that would cause physical, mental, or spiritual discomfort or hardship. While their intentions were good, the results have been catastrophic. A large part of this generation now believes they are something they are not. They overvalue who they are.

Once the children reach adulthood and the parent-protection bubble bursts, the reality of how the world sees them comes crashing down on them. No one is hovering over them to remove obstacles anymore. In fact, they face obstacles and problems purposely placed in front of them for them to solve and overcome on their own. The word to describe this new challenge is an old term: *work*. Businesses and bosses are not interested in coddling an influencer. They value results, and results require hardworking people. This requires characteristics that can only be forged in the fire of trial and suffering. The first chapter of James in the Bible talks about how trials that test your faith produce perseverance, which results in being mature and complete. That means the opposite is also true. No trials will result in no perseverance, no maturity, and no completeness. What once was a problem of overvaluing oneself can quickly become a problem of undervaluing oneself.

I believe a majority of the population is either neutral about their value as an individual or they undervalue what they have to offer.

Paul, the author of much of the New Testament, paid close attention to the importance of each person understanding and leaning into their value. He knew this principle was critical if the fledgling Christian movement was going to be able to spread and sustain momentum. If the early followers of Christ had thought they had little to no value in helping spread the gospel of Jesus and had settled into spectator status, expecting gifted orators to do all the work, the movement would have been dead in the water. The Roman government would have rounded up the Christian celebrities and thrown them in prison or executed them. All the masses of ordinary spectators would have gone home and proceeded with their ordinary lives. The problem posed by the pesky Jesus movement would have been immediately solved.

Spectators never start or grow anything. They just spectate. As soon as the object of their spectating is removed, they fade into the crowd.

In fact, the Roman government did try to round up and eliminate the leaders of the Jesus movement, and they failed miserably. Instead, the gospel of Jesus burst out of the tiny, backwater province of Israel on the edge of the Roman Empire and swept across the entire known world with breathtaking speed.

The movement was not made up of spectators. Paul's initial letters helped unite and encourage thousands of ordinary followers in his time and hundreds of millions since then to the very day you are reading this book.

> Spectators never start or grow anything. They just spectate.

You can feel the passion for value in the stroke of each word Paul wrote on that ancient parchment:

> Now as we have many parts in one body, and all the parts do not have the same function, in the same way we who are many are one body in Christ and individually members of one another. According to the grace given to us, we have different gifts: If prophecy, use it according to the proportion of one's faith. (Rom. 12:4–6)

> Indeed, the body is not one part but many. If the foot should say, "Because I'm not a hand, I don't belong to the body," it is not for that reason any less a part of the body. And if the ear should say, "Because I'm not an eye, I don't belong to the body," it is not for that reason any less a part of the body. If the whole body were an eye, where would the hearing be? If the

whole body were an ear, where would the sense of smell be? But as it is, God has arranged each one of the parts in the body just as he wanted. And if they were all the same part, where would the body be? As it is, there are many parts, but one body. The eye cannot say to the hand, "I don't need you!" Or again, the head can't say to the feet, "I don't need you!" On the contrary, those parts of the body that are weaker are indispensable. And those parts of the body that we consider less honorable, we clothe these with greater honor, and our unrespectable parts are treated with greater respect, which our respectable parts do not need.

Instead, God has put the body together, giving greater honor to the less honorable, so that there would be no division in the body, but that the members would have the same concern for each other. So if one member suffers, all the members suffer with it; if one member is honored, all the members rejoice with it.

Now you are the body of Christ, and individual members of it. (1 Cor. 12:14–27)

Just think if you were in the audience of those early followers listening to these words spoken directly to you. You would have felt them embedding themselves into your heart and taking root. *You have immense value, and you are part of a body of people that is changing the world!* No wonder this movement shook the Roman Empire and turned the world upside down!

Every part, regardless of function, is of equally extreme value to the body. That message contains the same accelerant today. This is amazing news for all of us who make up the ordinary parts of the body! We have inherent value not because of our form or function or abilities. It is because of the value placed on us by our Creator who knit us together in our mother's womb for a specific purpose on this earth for such a time as this!

Crippled

While individual value was critical to the breakout of Christianity in its infancy, the multitude of ways for people to access the projected lives of other people today though social and broadcast media has released the crippling disease of comparison on the masses. The symptoms of this devastating disease are easy to detect:

- Doubt—Compared to how awesome everyone else is, what do I possibly have to offer? What difference can I make?
- Fear—Compared to how awesome everyone else is, what if I try to be awesome and fail?
- Acceptance—Compared to how awesome everyone else is, I will never be that awesome. That is my lot in life.

The Bible is full of epic stories of thrilling victories and devastating defeats. One of those stories chronicles the release of the Hebrews from slavery in Egypt.

Their leader, Moses, led them on an amazing, harrowing journey toward a new land flowing with milk and honey. Along the way they got a front-row seat to the awesome power of God to deliver them and provide for their every need. He walked them directly out of institutional slavery after the plagues He released on the nation of Egypt. He defeated the entire Egyptian army hot on their heels by drowning them in a sea He had just split in half so the defenseless Hebrews could walk through untouched. He guided them along the way, appearing among them in the form of a pillar of fire at night and a cloud by day. When they got hungry out in the desert, no problem. He dropped meat out of the sky in the form of delicious quail flying directly into their camp each and every day. I've hunted quail before, but this was different. The quail hunted them! What chef would provide meat without some mouth-watering bread? Manna bread would form on the ground each and every day ready to be paired and plated for a delightful presentation that would make the producers of the Food Network envious. The availability of water is paramount to any living organism surviving in the searing heat of the desert. God split a rock and out came cold, pure water flowing to His people and animals headed to the land He promised them.

If you don't get the picture yet, it should start to become clear. God is awesome. He had chosen this group of people out of all the people in the world to be major characters in His redemptive story. The story starts at creation and the fall, moves toward the coming of Jesus Christ as Messiah, and ends with a grand finale curtain call featuring Satan and his followers thrown into hell and the followers of Jesus living together in heaven forever.

The chosen people of God should have been full of momentum and confidence in the awesomeness of God. He chose them! He had placed great value on them. Not because they were awesome but because they were created in His image and He already loved them. He didn't need them to be awesome. In contrast to their awesome God, every one of them was incredibly ordinary. There is great freedom in that fact. They didn't have to be awesome; they simply needed to be obedient. Therein lay their value.

But that is not what happened. As soon as their toes got to the edge of the Promised Land and they sent their spies out to get an assessment of the land God had already given them, something curious occurred. The report came back describing large people and large fortified cities. With their recent experiences of the awesomeness of God fresh in their minds, you would think they would have responded to the report with, "Yeah, so what?" and confidently marched into the land. But what should have been their natural movement was hindered.

You see, that is what a crippling disease does. It slows or removes the ability for natural movement. When they focused solely on the size of the people and fortifications, the crippling disease of comparison swept through the camp. They lost sight of how incredibly valuable they were because they were ordinary, but their God was extraordinary. This disease guided them back to their former slavery mind-set marked by seeing little to no value in themselves, destined to a life void of epic victory stories against overwhelming odds.

The crippling disease of comparison will still allow you to be somewhat active but not at the healthy level for which you were created.

Jesus is no stranger to crippling diseases. He was famous for healing people to display His divine power and prove that He was indeed the Son of God. He healed people who couldn't walk, who couldn't see, those who were sick and even dead!

The key thing to understand here is that when Jesus intersected with people who were crippled by some form of disease or physical need and healed them, He did not make them into some awesome superhuman specimen. He restored their bodies back to their normal function. He made them ordinary. Once they became ordinary, many of them would immediately join the movement of God, helping it to become known as a movement that was turning the world upside down. The doubt of what they had to offer dissipated. The fear was gone, they were ordinary, and that was awesome! They no longer had to accept their limited lot in life; they were now whole, and they wanted to tell everyone who would listen all about it.

Great movements that change things are not borne on the back of awesome; they are borne on the back of ordinary.

The good news if you have the symptoms of the crippling disease of comparison is this: there is a prescription. And it's simple: *Stop comparing.*

As I mentioned in an earlier chapter, I started to see the transformative power of value in new and deeply moving ways as I watched over my herd of trucks. The crippling disease of comparison had been healed, and I started to rejoice that I was ordinary. I became more keenly aware of it in other areas of culture and life.

A gathering storm would soon sweep across the business landscape, changing everything in its path. It would challenge widely accepted beliefs and traditions in a short amount of time. Business empires would rise and fall. In the middle of this chaos were some key indicators that could help guide churches and other organizations toward a new way of engaging and winning in the culture, and it all had to do with valuing the ordinary.

RECAP

Placing high value and expectations on volunteers to achieve an epic goal will surface and galvanize assets that already exist in the community to help create movement.

Organizations are not the only ones that need to value the ordinary individual. Individuals need to value themselves. If their own value of themselves is low, it will be difficult for them to ever reach high.

Comparing yourself to others can cause you to lose sight of your true value and cripple your influence.

Great movements that change things are not borne on the back of awesome; they are borne on the back of ordinary.

CHAPTER 5

MILLIONS OF TENS

The Long Tail

If you own a retail store, you know you have only a limited amount of shelf space to display products for sale in your store. Since you would want to make as much money as possible, you place the products with the highest demand ("the hits") on that limited shelf space. This increases your chance of moving inventory and increasing revenue.

It would be crazy to place items on your limited shelf space that aren't in high demand, wouldn't it? That would not be profitable. You would want "the hits" on your shelves at all times, right?

This retail strategy is based on scarcity. But what if you had unlimited shelf space which cost you next to nothing? What if you could still stock those same limited shelves with "the hits" but add thousands of other products that were not in such high demand on your new unlimited shelf space? Would you be interested in offering this massive amount of "nonhit items" to motivated, unique buyers who would eagerly purchase a few of each item? Of course you would!

This retail strategy is based on abundance.

This is not a "what if" discussion. This is exactly what happened in retail once the Internet was introduced, creating unlimited virtual shelf space in a globalized marketplace. I only need to mention the name of one company for you to get an idea of how successful it is to offer a large number of unique items with only a few items sold of each while also selling a few popular items in large quantities. That company is Amazon.

What I just described is a term called "The Long Tail" made popular by Chris Anderson in his book *The Long Tail: Why the Future of Business Is Selling Less of More*.[3]

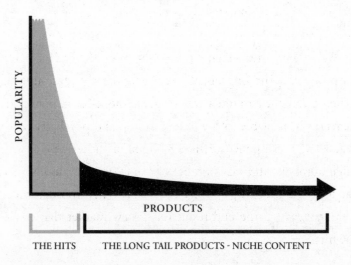

THE HITS   THE LONG TAIL PRODUCTS - NICHE CONTENT

---

[3] Chris Anderson, *The Long Tail: Why the Future of Business Is Selling Less of More* (Brentwood, TN: Hatchette Books, 2008).

The long tail effect states that you can earn as much or even more than the usual profits if you appeal and cater to the niche markets instead of just the broad market.

When you look at a graph that indicates the number of products sold and the highest ranking of those products, you can see a pattern form. The fewer, most popular items that sell the highest quantities are located at "the head" of the graph. The demand curve quickly drops to indicate the number of less popular items that sell the lesser number of products. That long line is referred to as "the tail" of the graph.

Anderson noticed that when you closely examine that long tail, you see that it doesn't contain any of the items that sell massive amounts. Those are the top ranked "hits" found in the head of the graph. But the items ranked lower that sell only a few items represent unique interests of niche markets, and the tail of that line is long. Could it be that all of those niche item purchases added up represent a significant amount of revenue?

When he examined emerging companies that had embraced the products in the long tail, he discovered something astounding. When a company found a way to make the lesser-known niche items easily available to the public to find and purchase, that is exactly what happened. Although none of those items sold in huge numbers, the vast number of niche products available in the long tail added up to huge numbers. When those numbers were aggregated, the end result was a new market that rivaled the hits.

Companies that Get It

Joe Kraus, CEO of JotSpot, commented on this emerging truth, "Up until now, the focus has been on dozens of markets of millions, instead of millions of markets of dozens."[4]

Examples of visionary companies that have emerged at an astronomical pace not only to reinvent their marketplace but to dominate it are Netflix and Amazon. Both were early adopters and quickly built systems to help customers navigate the long tail to find what they wanted. The sales of products they offered that were not available on the limited shelf space of their brick and mortar competitors amounted to between a quarter and nearly half of their total revenues, and that percentage continues to rise each year. An example of a media company that failed to embrace the concept of the long tail is Blockbuster. They had cornered the physical stores and shelf space and enjoyed an era of scarcity that forced everyone into their stores. Those stores no longer belong to Blockbuster. The speed of their demise due to the age of abundance was breathtaking and should send a stark message to modern churches.

In 2005, a new start-up called YouTube created a platform where amateurs could produce and display any type of moving image that interested them. It was a long tail on steroids featuring amateur niche videos. These were not professional production crews producing slick, elite videos for the entire population. This was a space for ordinary people to display their individual niche interests using emerging basic video editing tools made

---

[4] Anderson, *The Long Tail,* 209–10.

available to the masses. Its success has led to a site that now reaches more adults ages eighteen to thirty-four than any cable network with one billion unique monthly visitors and over six billion hours of video viewed every month. It eventually sold to Google for $1.65 billion, and current revenue estimates are listed at over $15 billion.

It is no longer the "hits" that rule. Suddenly the amateurs have a voice. They now go head to head with the professionals, and they often win.

In a *USA Today* article titled "Social Media Stars Flock to Old-School Retailers," Charisse Jones writes about the shifting landscape of marketing for traditional retail giants. The article mentions how Walmart, the world's biggest retailer, had embraced a six-year-old YouTube star to reach millions of other children with its products. The reason for their plan was compelling.

Ryan Toys Review is a children's YouTube channel that features Ryan Kaji along with his mother (Loann Kaji), father (Shion Kaji), and twin sisters (Emma and Kate). The daily videos basically feature him unboxing and playing with lots of toys. One of the channel's videos, "Huge Eggs Surprise Toys Challenge," has more than 1.8 billion views as of August 2019, making it the fortieth most viewed video on YouTube.[5] As of August 2019, Ryan Toys Review has more than twenty million subscribers, and the videos have garnered more than thirty

---

[5] "Huge Eggs Surprise Toys Challenge Inflatable Water Slide," YouTube, accessed February 2, 2018, https://www.youtube.com /watch?v=jjd-BeTX6U0.

billion views. The channel is rated as a Top 100 most subscribed YouTube channel in United States.[6]

According to *Forbes* magazine, in 2016–2017 Ryan was the eighth highest paid YouTube entrepreneur, having brought in $11 million in revenue between 2016 and 2017. In 2018 he was listed as the highest paid YouTuber bringing in $22 million of revenue from his videos and his product line at Walmart.

Jones went on to comment:

> Initially, it was mostly smaller brands, eager to make their mark in the world of e-commerce, that tended to turn to personalities on YouTube and Instagram for attention. But old school retailers are also recognizing that when it comes to connecting with Generations Y and Z, whose household spending is in the billions of dollars, a recommendation from someone they relate to can have far more sway than that of an actor or pop star. Research conducted in 2016 by influencer marketing firm Collective Bias, which is now owned by tech company Inmar, found 30 percent of shoppers were more inclined to buy a product endorsed by a blogger they viewed as a peer than a celebrity. And among those eighteen

---

[6] "Ryan Toys Review YouTube Channel Analytics and Report," accessed June 6, 2019, www.noxinfluencer.com.

to thirty-four years old, 70 percent preferred the noncelebrity.[7]

The seismic shift away from the exclusive hit-driven culture that has saturated society for the past half century is affecting everything that has embraced it. The population increasingly trusts and seeks insight from their peers more than corporate marketing machines when making purchasing decisions.

How business, entertainment, sports, churches, and nonprofits operate is being affected by this shift. But many in the culture are finding it difficult to adjust to this new normal. To understand why and what to do about it, you have to understand what built this culture in the first place.

The Hit Roller Coaster

Before the industrial revolution, the culture was primarily local and based on an agrarian economy. Pockets of culture were marked by local accents, music, and a variety of other traditions. Culture was splintered due to the lack of communication and transportation quickly interlocking dispersed communities. This resulted in a niche culture based on geographic separation.

There was a reason the church was the main mass cultural unifier in Western Europe: it had the best distribution infrastructure and, thanks to Gutenberg's press, the most mass-produced medium (the Bible).[8]

---

[7] Charisse Jones, "Social Media Stars Flock to Old-School Retailers, *USA Today* (August 6, 2018).

[8] Anderson, *The Long Tail,* 27.

This all changed with the rapid advancement of technological inventions. The first photographic process—heliography—was invented around 1824 by Nicéphore Niépce. In 1876, Thomas Edison established his first laboratory facility in Menlo Park, New Jersey, where he soon developed the phonograph as well as the first motion picture camera.

These inventions became the portal through which the dawn of the celebrity-age would emerge. For the first time cultural images, music, and movies could be distributed to widely dispersed audiences resulting in a unified spectator society.

Television broadcasting soon became the cultural glue that connected the country in a synchronized tapestry of entertainment and news. Radio climbed to great heights as well, seen in the famous fireside chats used by President Franklin Delano Roosevelt to unite millions of Americans around his policies and provide calm reassurance during World War II.

The dawn of "the hit" had emerged, which saw the niche, agrarian culture give way to the age of a one-size-fits-all, industrial culture. The population became obsessed with celebrity, and broadcast companies fed that obsession with a limited number of regularly scheduled entertainment and news outlets accessed by a majority of the country each evening. This cultural shift affected all aspects of society.

We became a hit-driven economy. The physical store shelves that housed all the inventory had limited space. Therefore, the owners wanted to stock those shelves with the items representing the highest demand, "the hits." Everything was based on scarcity.

As Anderson put it, we became a "lockstep culture."[9] The Hollywood blockbuster that began eight decades ago became the cultural fuel that took us to the celebrity-craved society we see today.

My grandfather played seven years in the NFL before the modern era of sports broadcasting. He never could have imagined what the NFL viewing landscape would become. In the early days of sports broadcasting, local sports coverage would be featured in a three-to-five-minute segment of the evening news. Since that time frame was limited, only the most popular local high school, college, and professional sports teams could be covered. The collegiate and professional league games and major sporting events were broadcast only on the weekends on one of three channels. This would feature local and regional teams and some nationally televised contests between the most popular teams (the hits).

As a young sports fan in rural Oklahoma, I remember watching primarily three professional teams with my dad on our one TV set featuring a shiny rabbit-ear antenna in our shag carpet living room. Throughout the year on Sunday afternoons, we tuned in to watch the Dallas Cowboys, Boston Celtics, and New York Yankees. They represented the sports hits in our area that were the most popular and brought in the most revenue. It wasn't that there were no other games being played throughout the year; it was just that we didn't have access to watch them. It was a time of scarcity in sports programming.

---

[9] Anderson, *The Long Tail*, 29.

That all changed in the 1980s with the creation of a new cable network dedicated entirely to sports programming. In 1979 the upstart 24-7 sports cable network called ESPN debuted, featuring everything from the major sporting events to the rarest of competitive sporting events. ESPN has since grown into a massive multiplexed network, with multiple channels as well as a huge news bureau that has led to the network bestowing the title of "Worldwide Leader in Sports" upon itself.

In 1970, a television executive named Roone Arledge rebelled against the conventional broadcast industry assumption that women controlled the TV set watching habits in the evening. If this assumption were true, then a football game aired in the evening during the week had little to no chance of being watched because it was assumed that women didn't watch pro football. This was one of the main reasons the limited NFL games that were broadcast on TV were only offered on one day during one time of the week, Sunday afternoon. When ABC won the broadcasting rights, Arledge unveiled a cutting-edge sports program called *Monday Night Football*. It was an immediate success and continues to expand as an iconic cultural event to now include *Thursday Night Football*.

The world of sports broadcasting is now one of abundance. Sports fans have access to a massive number of games in practically every sport from which they can choose to view on a variety of TVs, tablets, and mobile devices. Gone are the days of scarcity where fans had to go to a stadium to view a game or have a game chosen for them to view on TV once a week. Now the stadium comes to the fans, and they get to choose which ones they want to watch and when they want to watch them.

When it comes to sports broadcasting, it is no longer one-size-fits-all; it is all sizes fit one.

We have reentered a society that is marked more by the niche than one-size-fits-all.

In a 2005 speech, News Corp chairman Rupert Murdoch showed that he was among the first of the media moguls to grasp the magnitude of today's elite versus amateur divide: "Young people don't want to rely on a Godlike figure from above to tell them what's important," he said. "They want control over their media, instead of being controlled by it."[10]

We entered the realm of abundance.

Every hit *and* niche product could be made available to everyone at any time without the scarcity of limited physical shelf space. It has provided the opportunity for any and all people who were formerly consumers to now become producers. A majority of these new producers are not interested in being a celebrity; they simply do it because they love it.

Understanding the rise and fall of the hit is critical to understanding the value of the ordinary and positioning ministries and organizations to flourish in the twenty-first century and beyond.

Understand the Times

All businesses, churches, and other organizations are a reflection of the culture in which they operate. In fact, if they don't understand how to read and react to the culture in which

---

[10] Anderson, *The Long Tail*, 37.

they live, they will fail. So it makes sense that the hit-driven culture that marked the past eight decades would become part of the canvas of every organization. This is what connected people; it was what people were comfortable with each day. It wasn't necessarily bad; it was just the way it was.

The "hit" culture expressed itself in the church with the parishioners bestowing celebrity status to the professional ministers within the lockstep culture of the pews. The church staff were considered "the hits"—the most talented, gifted orators and theologically educated that occupied the scarce shelf space of the podium and the pulpit. The amateurs were tasked with helping out with the church programs and inviting people to experience "the hits." The communities were part of a lockstep culture that didn't have an abundance of things vying for their time, which made the positive fellowship and community found at church attractive. Plus, you could hear an inspiring message from a ministry expert before heading home for fried chicken and the one game you were allowed to watch (as determined by the broadcast experts).

It was the era of scarcity that featured the experts and the culture that followed their every demand. It wasn't necessarily bad; it was just the way it was.

But that's no longer the way it is.

When cultural shifts happen, churches, nonprofits, and businesses can either adjust and ride the new wave toward new and effective ministries that will impact the world or stay the course of the past and be crushed by that same wave.

But how could we adjust? The story of Josiah gathering people together in one place and reading them the Bible, along with the emerging shift in the business landscape, had opened my eyes to a potential problem of valuing programs and the "hits" over ordinary people.

I had an idea that I thought could solve that problem and unleash hidden influence. The path forward wasn't crystal clear, but I knew what the next step would be. I didn't want to move forward until I received wise counsel from experienced leaders who had been on the front lines, so I made a list of ministry and business professionals and began scheduling times to run my idea by them and get their input. I thought I would receive a resounding and unifying response that would make it easy to move forward. What I found is that innovative thoughts always emerge out of the fog where status quo intersects with what could be but is yet unseen.

My discussions would both confirm my suspicions and instill doubt in my idea. I realized there would have to be faith in what was unseen in order to move forward.

The Hook

"It will never work" was the statement that echoed in my head. Their responses were mixed, as was the confidence I now had in my idea.

The idea? Have people meet together at one of the only remaining locations that unite communities regardless of race, socioeconomic status, gender, politics, etc. The location was an athletic field.

The next thought was the one that caused everyone to pause. I wanted to follow the Josiah principle of joining everyone together in one place and putting people up front that weren't considered to be professional ministry leaders. They would be ordinary young leaders committed to the Word of God and following Jesus.

A majority of those I talked to were uncomfortable with this proposition. They believed that giving the mic to young, untrained teenagers would destroy the event. The prevailing thought at that time was that teenagers needed something to keep their attention. They required something "entertaining."

Where did this idea come from? It was the culture of "the hit" rearing its ugly head again. Ministry leaders were nervous about creating an outdoor event that featured an amateur at the mic. Why? Well, everyone was convinced that the general population only responded to the celebrity. And make no bones about it, there was a celebrity culture in the Christian world, and there still is. These were the gifted adult speakers and orators along with the talented worship leaders and recording artists. Everyone was convinced that if you got a crowd together, these aspects needed to be there to keep the crowd's attention. No celebrity? No attention. That was the culture.

What I was proposing was radical. Identify and pursue the ordinary and give them the mic.

"What are you going to do if it rains?" was another question I often got. My response was that I would encourage the event organizer to also reserve a gym so they could move the event indoors. Many of my advisors indicated that this would be even worse. You see, an indoor gym is not built with sound dynamics in mind. Basically, sound bounces everywhere in a gym. If experienced speakers had a difficult time keeping students' attention in gymnasiums, just think how bad the outcome would be if an untrained, ordinary teenager were thrust in front of the same attention-deficit-disorder mob. The crowd would start talking to one another, rolling their eyes, and disconnecting within minutes. The noise and movement would be unbearable, resulting in the poor, isolated teenager at the mic feeling alone and humiliated. The event would quickly descend into disaster.

I was advised over and over with this truth: "You need a hook."

What was "a hook"? It was "the hit," the professional speaker who could quickly capture and keep the attention of a large crowd of teenagers gathered in one place to hear something about God. No different than a hook with a fish. It was this bedrock belief that had spawned the dizzying array of ministry tactics that had grown into universally accepted programmatic doctrine. Massive pizza parties; high-tech, high-octane concerts, camps and conferences; big personality youth pastors and speakers; captivating, emotional testimonies from the adults.

Read and React

If we want our ministries to penetrate the culture, we have to understand and navigate the culture, which is constantly changing. What was the culture I was navigating? It was none other than the hit-driven culture that had erupted onto the scene over the decades since the industrial revolution.

It was difficult to match the Hollywood-fueled celebrity fanaticism that had taken over the nation, but we were doing our best. Churches struggled to match the hit culture that had been embraced by every facet of society. High value was placed on the experts; those who could communicate best became the most popular. It was increasingly difficult to get a crowd together in one place for an event. Only a limited number of events could be pulled off; therefore, you had to put your best on the stage.

This was a strategy based on scarcity. No different from the retail strategy based on limited shelf space. After all, that is what the hit-driven culture expected. Only the best made it to the shelf for people to buy, and the trained, professional ministers were considered the expert or the hit.

What about everybody else? What about all the nonhits? The message to them was loud and clear: *you have no value.* If they had any, it was only in inviting the other valueless spectators.

What emerged was a culture of professional, trained experts on the stage with the rest of the church relegated to inviting their friends to hear those experts. Again, this wasn't necessarily wrong; it was just the way it was. Many people had their lives impacted for eternity, and God moved in incredible ways through His people.

But cracks were starting to show in that strategy.

At this point I found myself confronted with the difficult decision of choosing between the overwhelming conventional ministry wisdom of needing a "hook" versus featuring ordinary members of the "long tail" to deliver the same message in a new way. I could not remember a youth ministry event I or anyone else had done that featured the untrained, ordinary student as the main speaker, what I called the "hero" of the program. Many times we tend to think of a hero as someone almost superhuman who accomplishes amazing feats. But most heroes are simply people who do the right thing at the right time, regardless of the challenge.

The battle with doubt had begun. What would happen if we scheduled this event without featuring a celebrity? Would anyone even come? And if they did, would they even have the capacity or ability to listen to someone who wasn't a raving hit?

There was only one way to find out. We were going to run the play Josiah did centuries before and see what God would do.

I would like to say I was extremely confident of success, but truthfully, I was struggling to move forward in the face and reality of the culture. I had no idea what God had in store. He extended enough patience and grace to allow me a front-row seat to see what would happen when an event was planned that had no chance of success unless God showed up and used the untrained, ordinary in an extraordinary way.

God is never surprised or confused by the current state of the culture and where it is headed. We simply need to listen and follow His lead.

Instead of thinking tens of millions, we needed to start thinking millions of tens. The culture was shifting away from the masses allowing the few experts to determine what the hits were and toward the rise of ordinary producers given a voice in the abundance of the long tail. It was time for the church to understand the times. Perhaps placing success or failure on ordinary teenagers—not gifted adults—by giving them a microphone and a platform to be heard on a field in their community would activate one of the greatest motivators in the depths of the human spirit—value.

Would they respond as the spectators they had been relegated to over the past decades? Or would something well up deep inside of them that had been there all along—the feeling that they were never meant to be just spectators?

RECAP

Our culture has changed. The long tail reveals the power of the combined influence of ordinary, niche producers.

We need to stop thinking of tens of millions and start thinking of millions of tens.

We are no longer a lockstep culture dominated by "the hits."

CHAPTER 6

DOLLARS AND CORDS

Trust

I recently attended a conference in Zurich, Switzerland, and met Mike Zurbrugg, cofounder of Shine Europe, a youth ministry designed to help build youth movements in every country of Western Europe so that every teen will know someone who follows Jesus.

The movement has been experiencing great results in Western Europe among teenagers. Mike shared insights at the conference that eerily reflected the same thing I had experienced when it came to one of the keys to establishing movement among teenagers:

> Everyone teaches, teaches, teaches. We challenge. We send them now. When they fall and

ask for help, we are there to coach. If we just
teach, they sit back and get on their phones.
When you give them big challenges and
momentum, they get going. They do it because
we expect it. They know we take them serious.
We treat them like adults. We motivate, and
motivation is more fun. You elevate what works,
and when you elevate the teenagers to lead, you
communicate that you believe they are valuable.

I asked Mike over lunch what the biggest change is that
churches and organizations need to make to adopt this strategy.
He answered, "The biggest change is to trust teenagers." In fact,
a printed brochure explaining what the Shine Ministry is all
about has this statement in bold letters filling up an entire page:
"We don't train and teach to death, but we trust in youth to do
great things."

This had been a barrier that had limited the inherent
influence in every volunteer and teenager for decades. You don't
value what you don't trust. One way to reinforce that you don't
value volunteers or youth is not to "trust in youth to do great
things."

One student expressed this truth at a recent National
Campus Summit I attended that included leaders from more
than sixty of the largest youth organizations in America. When
asked what one idea she would give to those in attendance to
ignite a youth movement, she said, "Stop sugarcoating things for
us. Challenge us to do great things and help us do them!"

Trust You Can Touch

Trust and value have been keys to empowering the students that have led Fields of Faith over the years. It was practically expressed by giving them the microphone and the spotlight on the stage. They knew they were being taken seriously, and they responded in remarkable ways.

The following examples show how this principle can be practically expressed in a variety of ways across all industries and professions.

Puttin' on the Ritz

The founder and owner of the Ritz Carlton, Horst Schulze, expressed the empowering principle of trust in the following way. He established a policy that stated the following: Every employee, from the general manager down to the newest busboy, is empowered to spend up to $2,000 to make sure the guest is happy.[11] No increase in their activity, just increased ability and authority to make an empowered command decision as they carried out the normal responsibilities of their job. They didn't need to wait for permission from on high. They were trusted to make the call as they saw fit. This policy reflects a core belief that Schulze has about his employees, "We're not designed to flounder aimlessly through life. We're hardwired to want to do something of value. . . . We've been programmed to seek to

---

[11] Horst Shultze, *Excellence Wins: A No-Nonsense Guide to Becoming the Best in a World of Compromise* (Grand Rapids: Zondervan, 2019).

achieve in some area so we can look back with pride and say, 'I did that.'"[12]

Andon

With all the complex engineering and moving parts of an automobile assembly line, a simple rope above the line can go unnoticed. It is easy to miss. The rope seems out of place in the high-tech production process infused with artificial intelligence and pinpoint systems built for speed and efficiency. But this is not just any rope. It contains great strength, which lies not in what it can do but in who can do it.

It is called an Andon Cord, and it was introduced to the Toyota assembly process by Taiichi Ohno. He gave every employee on the assembly line the ability and authority to pull the cord and stop the entire production line if they detected anything that would affect overall quality. When they pulled that cord, they weren't just asking for permission to stop the line; they were actually stopping the line.

Bestowing that level of authority on ordinary line workers was unheard of at the time. It seemed crazy. Not only did the world's carmakers not believe the people assembling their products had enough judgment to make that call, but it was expensive to stop the entire process. People thought it would cost more than it would save.

The benefits, however, far outweighed the risks. As line workers identified issues, they were able to assess the root cause

---

and come up with immediate countermeasures to address the problem before it became more embedded and widespread down the line.

In the short run production decreased, but the quality increased. In the long run less time was spent trying to identify problems in the production line and repairing thousands of cars that made it through the process and into the hands of now unsatisfied customers. The Andon Cord had made the Toyota production line more efficient, not less.

This bold move paid off. Toyota became a global automotive juggernaut.

Think how the workers on the production line felt when the highest level of leadership in their company bestowed upon them the ability to halt production in an industry that was predicated on keeping the production line moving at all costs. If the line isn't moving, money is being lost. Estimates of stopping the production line were that it cost $15,000 per minute.

Instead of being considered simple participants in a process, they knew they were considered to be highly trusted and valued team members who were empowered to make key quality assurance decisions based on their own judgment. This contributed to a heightened culture of shared ownership and pride in the output of the company's product. Their engagement and performance soared.

Was there an increased level of risk for the company to entrust so much to the ordinary line worker? Absolutely. Was the challenge increased to the line workers to make high level decisions? Definitely. But the principle of value had unlocked the untapped influence that resided in each worker, which flowed out through the entire organization.

RECAP

Trust your people to do great things.

Take a risk. Be bold to empower your volunteers and employees with increased ability and authority in their position. Engagement and performance will soar.

PART 3

SIMPLICITY

It is better to teach one idea to hundreds
of people than hundreds of ideas to one.

AFRICAN PROVERB

CHAPTER 7

SIMPLIFY TO MAXIMIZE

The Spark

Complexity kills movement.

Lucas Ramirez states, "The truth is that complex order does not necessarily come from complex behavior or thought."[1] If we wanted to start a movement that focused on volunteers as the primary lynchpin, we had to keep everything simple.

It seemed like every youth program idea that came along was always accompanied by thick training manuals, videos, and resources with the program brand emblazoned on every promotional product known to man. By the time all of these resources were deployed, volunteers weren't sure what to do

---

[1] Lucas Ramirez, *Designed for More: Unleashing Christ's Vision for Unity in a Deeply Divided World* (Nashville: FaithWords, 2018).

next. But as ministers, it made us feel good that we had "blessed" them with our awesome ministry resources when we had actually buried them under an avalanche of information. Most content creators are thinking of transferring their ideas and strategies in print and digital form. They have plenty of time to think about their projects and are passionate about them. Few of them are thinking of creating movement through a valued volunteer leader on the front lines of life. If deployment of program content, curriculum, and resources was the measure of success, we had won. But if creating a movement to change people and impact the culture was the measure, well, that was a different story few leaders wanted to talk about.

I read a fascinating book that is now out of print titled *Two Ears of Corn*.[2] The main thesis of the book was based on how to increase food production capacity in third-world agricultural economies. The premise was how to move from growing one ear of corn to two ears of corn. The author railed against the tendencies of first-world nations imposing their advanced farming technology, training, and talent on third-world farmers that had no idea how to apply the resources successfully. The amount of information, training, and infrastructure support needed was overwhelming, so as soon as the experts left, they would set it aside, let it rust, and keep doing what they had done for centuries. Instead of asking the farmers what they needed and introducing one or two steps that would help them in what they were already doing, the "experts" deployed complex,

---

[2] Roland Bunch, *Two Ears of Corn: A Guide to People-Centered Agricultural Improvement* (Oklahoma City: World Neighbors, 1995).

interconnected technology and advanced training that wasted everyone's time and money. As John W. Mellor writes, "A high proportion of success stories tend to involve innovations which were very similar to practices already followed, which were simple and easy to apply, and which provided unusually high returns."[3]

> If complexity can kill a movement, then simplicity can spark a movement.

There's nothing more inspiring than seeing a $500,000 combine tractor sitting in a village with chicken wire wrapped around it being used as a chicken coop!

I knew that going forward we had to be committed to maintaining simplicity with what we were asking from our highly valued volunteers. We needed to narrow the goal in order to widen the impact. If complexity can kill a movement, then simplicity can spark a movement.

This thought would soon be reinforced by a chance conversation with a military officer on leave from the wars in Iraq and Afghanistan.

Center of Gravity

Jeff Madison had always been a tough guy. In high school he earned the nickname "Maddog" from his aggressive play

---

[3] John W. Mellor, "The Subsistence Farmer in Traditional Economies," in Clifton R. Wharton Jr., ed., *Subsistence Agriculture and Economic Development* (Abingdon, Oxfordshire, England: Routledge, 2017), 221.

as the starting middle linebacker. He was always competing. When football was over, he wrestled. Once the wrestling season ended, it was time to grab the glove and bat and hit the baseball diamond.

Jeff married my sister Kathy and went on to graduate from college at the top of his ROTC class. He later became an elite member of the U.S. Army whose qualifications included Ranger and Master Parachutist. During his twenty-six-year military career, he served in a broad range of experiences including command and staff at many levels, armored cavalry scout, counterinsurgent in Afghanistan, resource manager in Europe, Provincial Reconstruction Leader in Iraq, and United Nations Peacekeeper in Israel and Egypt. Jeff ended his distinguished career at the rank of colonel. I was honored to be part of his retirement ceremony at the Pentagon.

Maddog had just returned from one of his many deployments to Iraq and Afghanistan. Our families joined forces in Dallas to visit Six Flags over Texas and give our kids a chance to enjoy the rides and shows while the adults baked in the hot Texas sun and rapidly drained our checking accounts.

While we were standing in line at the Roaring Rapids ride, I struck up a conversation with Maddog. There are a lot of similarities between the military and ministry. The Bible contains many military references. I was always curious to see what I could learn from a military officer that could possibly help me establish and expand my ministry.

I asked, "When you are approaching a town in combat, how do you go about overtaking it?" I was interested because I asked myself this question when I was driving to one of the many communities I served across southwest Oklahoma. I wanted to see Jesus Christ take over the town, and I wanted to know how God might use me to help make that a reality.

Maddog smiled and said, "Well, that's a little complex, and I'm not sure I can answer that before we get strapped into our ride. But the simple answer is to first identify the center of gravity. This can be a person, a political party, or even the will of the people. Once this is identified, you cut off or disrupt communication with the center of gravity. The final step is to invade."

The line for the ride moved but only slightly. Jeff was a devout follower of Jesus Christ, so I asked him a follow-up question.

"What would you say is the center of gravity for Christianity?"

He thought for a moment and replied, "It's Jesus Christ."

He was right. Colossians 1:15–17 says:

> He is the image of the invisible God,
> the firstborn over all creation.
> For everything was created by him,
> in heaven and on earth,
> the visible and the invisible,
> whether thrones or dominions
> or rulers or authorities—
> all things have been created through him and
> for him.
> He is before all things,
> and by him all things hold together.

I immediately asked another follow-up question, "How would you disrupt or cut off Christians from communicating with their center of gravity?" He furrowed his brow as he thought out loud through the tactics he would use. "I wouldn't be worried too much about a weekly church service, since that is just thirty to forty-five minutes of an entire week, same thing for small groups. And those environments are not direct communication; they are indirect."

The line we were standing in turned the corner, and we could see the ride—or what appeared to be the ride. (It could have been a mirage caused by the heat. I wasn't sure.)

Maddog finished his military assessment. "I would disrupt Christians from spending individual time reading their Bibles and praying. This is direct communication with the center of gravity that coordinates and inspires all their efforts. This can happen at any time of the day or night and doesn't depend on anyone else to execute. I would attack and destroy daily Bible reading and prayer."

I was quiet for a moment. "What would you do next?"

He stared right at me. "Invade."

The hair stood up on the back of my neck. I had not told him anything of my experience reading about Josiah. With military precision Maddog had just described what had been a key part in destroying Judah. A series of godless kings had cut off communication with God by removing the Scripture. A rebellious generation would leave the next generation without the Scripture, and they would have no idea how to follow God. Each generation would get worse. The enemies of God invaded and held ground for generations.

But there was a revival. A young king found the Scripture and reestablished communication with the center of gravity, Yahweh, the God of the Hebrews.

As we finally stepped onto the water ride, there was a burning question in my mind. Had Christians in America simply stopped reading the Word of God and grown content with just sitting in pews and listening to the professionals tell them about God?

If this were so, that would explain what was going on. Christianity was being invaded. The lines were being overrun, and we didn't even know the cause.

I had to find out.

The following week, I would be conducting a leadership workshop at the Oklahoma FCA Leadership Camp. This camp attracted the top Christian student athletes in the state. These were athletes who were in positions of leadership on their teams, on their campuses, in their communities, and in their churches. There couldn't be a better proving ground.

The leadership camp was sold out. The unique environment of equally yoked competitive athletes wanting to grow in their faith and leadership skills made it easy to pack out the camp.

My breakout session was scheduled for the second day. I was anxious to see what I would find out from these spiritual leaders who came from every corner of the state, as well as north Texas. I started my breakout session with 175 athlete leaders locked in and ready to increase their leadership capacity.

Before I got to my presentation, I asked a simple question: "How many of you spend time directly communicating with God through His Scripture on a consistent basis?"

I further qualified my question, "I'm not talking about listening to what your youth pastor or pastor teaches you about their communication with God. I'm not talking about what you have read in a devotional or a book about the author's communication with God. I'm not talking about worship songs that contain lyrics about God. I'm talking about you personally communicating with God on a consistent basis through His Word. Oh, and by the way, I need you to be brutally honest with your assessment of yourself. That is what great leaders do."

I looked out over the crowd for a brief moment to let the question settle in, "Now raise your hand if you directly communicate with God in this manner."

Of the packed room full of 175 of our best leaders, three of them sheepishly raised their hands. I felt a knot form in my stomach. This wasn't a conclusive scientific test, but it was indeed a compelling indicator.

I had to get more input. After camp was over, I started visiting youth ministers and asked them the same question about their youth. The universal reply time after time was that their youth were taught about "quiet times," but most of them did not spend consistent, personal time in God's Word.

It was becoming abundantly clear. The vast majority of youth involved in churches and parachurch organizations were attending and watching events that were organized and led by adults who were considered the God experts. If this were true in what was considered the "buckle of the Bible Belt," then it was even more prevalent beyond.

The only conclusion I could come to was that the leaders of Christianity in America had successfully created a *spectator generation* of Christian youth. These were good kids involved in highly entertaining programs led by highly skilled pastors and youth pastors, but their greatest communication opportunity with their center of gravity had been severely disrupted or effectively cut off. And no one seemed to realize it!

I could not get my earlier conversation with Maddog out of my head. The facts were undeniable. Our center of gravity had been identified by our enemy. Our communication with our center of gravity had been effectively disrupted and cut off. The final step was now happening all around us.

Invasion.

As ominous as this sounded, the Josiah strategy of reestablishing personal connection to the Word of God through the influence of a young leader was looming out there as a proven way to counterattack the invasion and turn the tide.

But there would have to be a fundamental change in the established Christian culture.

If it worked for Josiah, could the same strategy work today in our culture? I was ready to put this question to the test.

Critical Nodes

Over the years I've had the unique opportunity to talk with some of the world's experts on leading high-performing small teams and engaging overwhelming odds resulting in victory. I've recently had a chance to interact with some of the best—U.S. Navy Seals.

I would share with several of them the findings on the basics of taking over a town/city from my discussion with Colonel

Madison. I wanted to verify that what I understood from our conversation years before was correct and get their take on the basic tactical principles my brother-in-law had discussed.

Their response convinced me that we were applying a strategy that not only worked but was a threat to our ancient enemy. One of them sent me this email after our conversation about the center of gravity:

> Seal teams are small in size but large on disruption. . . . That is to say, we never engage a target blindly without information and intelligence. We never engage armored vehicles/positions without the proper firepower, whether with us or on call. And we never take out a whole system—meaning we attack "critical nodes" such as a single point of failure in a system which causes a cascade effect for shutting down the objective and surrounding infrastructure. Find the "critical nodes" and you will succeed.
>
> —Navy Seal Command Master Chief

The principal verified the strategy of disrupting the center of gravity. Find one simple part of the overall system you want to bring down and take it out, causing the whole system to fail.

Another Seal gave me an example of critical node theory. He said that if you don't have the ability to blow up the construction of a large bridge, you may be able to eliminate the supply of gasoline to the trucks delivering the concrete needed to build the bridge. Eliminating the critical node of gas supply effectively shuts down one part of the supply system, which then halts all construction, rendering the entire bridge useless.

This was the opposite of a complex, multilayered, and coordinated attack. Identify one simple, critical thing, and take it out.

I believe the Word of God is a critical node. What is a primary way each one of us can connect with God at any time to know who He is and how we are to live? The Bible.

What did Jesus quote to defeat Satan when He was tempted? The Bible.

It wasn't a devotional. In fact, if He wanted to just come up with His own new quotes, He could have done that, and it would have been the same as quoting the Bible. He was the Word of God in the flesh. Every word He uttered was divine! But He didn't do that. He modeled for us the power of the divine words of God captured in the written form of the Scriptures.

The Bible contains the words of God that change lives, families, communities, cultures, and countries. If it has that much impact, it is indeed a critical node, one that affects everything in our lives. It will be targeted by our enemy as a single point of failure in order to bring down a life, a marriage, a community, a culture, and a country.

RECAP

Complexity kills movement. Simplicity sparks movement.

Jesus is our center of gravity. Daily personal communication with Him is imperative.

The Bible is a critical node. When it is removed, it will have a cascading effect on all areas of our lives.

CHAPTER 8

THE TWO-EDGED SWORD

The Power of Four

> Read the Bible for instruction. Read it for inspi-
> ration. Read it for insight. Read it out of duty.
> Read it out of curiosity. Read it out of wonder.
> Whatever you do, read it. Not to read the Bible
> is to misunderstand God's mind and miss His
> heart. —Woodrow Kroll

A study was conducted that reinforced the findings I had
been compiling about the critical node of Scripture. The Center
of Bible Engagement compiled extensive research findings by
Arnold Cole, EdD, and Pamela Caudill Ovwigho, PhD, into

a document titled "Understanding the Bible Engagement Challenge: Scientific Evidence for the Power of 4."[4]

In the study, they polled forty thousand people ages eight to eighty. They wanted to see how people were engaging Scripture. As they compiled the results, they made a profound discovery they were not even looking for when they originally planned the survey.

The study indicated that when people engaged Scripture one time a week, which could include a pastor instructing the congregation to "open your Bibles," there was negligible effect on some key areas of their life. The same result was true if people engaged Scriptures two times a week. The result equaled little to no effect.

Three times a week saw a small indication of life. There was a slight pulse, a faint heartbeat. Something moved in the behavior of the person engaging Scripture.

The eye-opener happened when Bible engagement reached at least four times a week.

A steady climb of impact would have been expected, but that was not the case. The level was basically stagnant over days one and two, with a small bump on day three. But when day four was reached, the effects spiked in an astounding way. The stunning findings included the following:

[4] Arnold Cole, Ed.D., and Pamela Caudill Ovwigho, Ph.D., "Understanding the Bible Engagement Challenge: Scientific Evidence for the Power of 4," Center for Bible Engagement, December 2009, accessed September 22, 2020, https://bttbfiles.com/web/docs/cbe/Scientific_Evidence_for_the_Power_of_4.pdf.

- Feeling lonely drops 30 percent
- Anger issues drop 32 percent
- Bitterness in relationships drops 40 percent
- Alcoholism drops 57 percent
- Sex outside of marriage drops 68 percent
- Feeling spiritually stagnant drops 60 percent
- Viewing pornography drops 61 percent
- Sharing your faith jumps 200 percent
- Discipling others jumps 230 percent

The research literally leaps off the charts. The findings hammer home the truth that there are profound differences between people who engage Scripture at least four times a week and those who engage Scripture less often.

This data is revealing. There is a full-blown effort to keep the followers of Christ from consistently reading the Bible on a daily basis. Colonel Madison would describe this as effectively cutting off the population from their center of gravity.

Integral to these findings is that people who engage the Bible one to three days a week indicate basically the same effect on their personal lives as those who do not engage at all. The deceptive reality is that they can feel good about their activities without any sustainable results. They think they're being "good Christians," but their lives are no different from people who aren't Christians at all.

This can be devastating to a movement. Limited activity is elevated to the same effect as consistent activity, when it is actually the same as no activity.

The reality is that with a lack of consistent Bible engagement defined as at least four times a week, Christians have less confidence in sharing their faith with others and are more vulnerable to falling prey to false teachings, as well as a lethargy and apathy in consistently living out their faith in their circle of influence.

The studies show that the best spiritually based predictor among thirteen- to seventeen-year-old teenagers was their engagement in Scripture. This verified what I originally felt when I got the honest feedback from the student-athlete leaders at our FCA leadership camp.

The other side of the coin is equally conclusive and encouraging. The more Christians read or listen to Scripture at least four times a week, the bolder they will be in sharing their faith and growing in their faith. Their lives will begin to have a profound impact on those immediately around them. There will also be fewer times of stagnation in their spiritual growth. They will become viral in their faith.

This mounting evidence of the impact of Scripture on not only the individuals in a society but to the actual underpinnings of an entire society can lead to the findings being discouraging when you find out that most people are not communicating to their center of gravity and are cut off, making them vulnerable to invasion. But the power of simplicity goes both ways. When a critical node is identified and reengaged, the entire system can be reinvigorated with astonishing and rapid effect. This is exactly the story of Josiah and it is the story of Fields of Faith.

There is an answer. There is hope. Just keep it simple.

Word to the People

It is a time of societal upheaval. The shifting tectonic plates of politics, religion, financial instability, social justice, war, and many other issues rumble in a dizzying array around people in many countries.

The unrest and unease are palpable, but no one can easily understand it all, much less explain what can be done about it. There are so many moving parts that it almost seems like everything is being communicated in a foreign language.

Well, in fact, it was.

This was the scenario that surrounded a young monk named Martin Luther in the early 1500s in Germany. It eventually led to a generation-defining moment of protest encapsulated in a piece of parchment pierced by a nail, passionately hammered into the front wooden door of a castle church in Wittenberg, Germany, in 1517.

The parchment contained ink that communicated what was titled the "95 Theses." These ninety-five revolutionary opinions contained the spark that would ignite the Protestant Reformation, which would go on to revolutionize Western civilization.

Many people had expressed the same sentiments for many years in a variety of locations throughout Europe. The difference in Luther is that he understood the principle of simplicity.

Most of his contemporaries would express their frustrations in lengthy academic pontifications. But Luther had an uncanny understanding of how to communicate with the ordinary German. He was able to navigate the use of new printing technology that created short, easily understandable pamphlets, which were cheap to make and simple to distribute.

Printing, before the Reformation, was only used for complex scholarly writings primarily by deceased authors in book form. Books were an expensive proposition that required a large up-front investment with no guarantee of any future sales. Luther's thoughts, captured on short, easily understandable writings in the language of the common German, were publishing dynamite. They took advantage of the new, emerging printing press technology in a way that limited publishing risk while exponentially raising the distribution and financial reach of the ordinary printing company.

Luther was driven by an insatiable desire to put the Bible in the hands of ordinary Christians across Germany in their own language. This was an act of open defiance to Rome. Before this radical action became a reality, the only available Scriptures were written in Latin, effectively making the Word of God accessible only to learned linguistic experts.

Think about what that would look like today. Currently, if you are curious about what the Word of God has to say about an issue, you have easy access to print and/or digital Bibles in a seemingly endless variety of styles and platforms. If you're in a hurry, you can google your question and be provided a plethora of suggested Scriptures in a variety of translations and languages sent directly to your phone.

This type of access would have been entirely foreign to basically all the Germanic peoples in the early 1500s. It was an accepted fact that only the clergy and academics of the time could access, read, and understand the Word of God. They were the only ones who could deliver the holy Scriptures to the poor, unfortunate, and unlearned population. The Bible had been successfully quarantined from the ordinary masses.

This was a foregone conclusion accepted by everyone until Luther came along with his radical belief that ordinary people should have direct access to the God of the Bible at any time of their own choosing. This belief was part of the fault line that began to shake an empire controlled by emperors, kings, and clergy, resulting in the eventual dismantling and reshaping of most of Western civilization. It was a colossal shift that could trace one of its primary sources directly to the act of translating the Scriptures into the language of ordinary people.

As my Navy Seal friends had emphasized, critical nodes are important. If you can clearly identify one and take it down, the entire system fails. But the opposite is also true: if you can effectively repair a critical node and protect it from further attack, the entire system comes back online and becomes a renewed threat.

It was becoming abundantly clear to me that the words of God contained in the Bible had been a critical node throughout history. When it was attacked and effectively eliminated, a cascading spiritual collapse always followed. When it was made available and understandable, spiritual awakening was possible.

If just compulsory reading of the Bible was the main prerequisite to be a true follower of Christ, then the Pharisees would have received high accolades from Jesus. But that was not the case. He called them whitewashed tombs, and they ultimately led the charge to kill Him. The type of Bible engagement God wants from us—the type that changes us—is a willing, humble, and obedient reading. When the Scriptures are engaged and consumed with this kind of willing, humble, and obedient heart, change happens.

The critical node of connection directly to our center of gravity engages with incredible effect. God's people begin to move in sync with His divine direction. A coordinated effort emerges that routs the enemy.

The Bible is not short of words that speak about this victory over the one who wants to cut us off from our center of gravity: "You are from God, little children, and you have conquered them, because the one who is in you is greater than the one who is in the world" (1 John 4:4).

I am deeply passionate about the critical nature of being saturated in the Word of God on a daily basis because it has changed my life. The words of God are a surge of nourishment to my soul. This isn't just an idea for me; it's my life.

When I was attending seminary, I started to realize something through the process of successfully completing my master of divinity degree. With every year that passed, I wasn't one year closer to knowing more about God. I actually was one year closer to realizing how little I knew about God. The more I learned, the more I saw the vastness of God and how little I could comprehend of who He is. I realized that the best chance I had to get to understand God and His divine plan for my life was to daily spend time with His words. Only then would I best know how to live my life, see what I needed to change and how to treat others.

Jesus described it like this: "I am the vine; you are the branches. The one who remains in me and I in him produces much fruit, because you can do nothing without me" (John 15:5).

When I am approached by staff who are new to ministry, they ask me a wide variety of questions about how to navigate the treacherous waters of ministering to broken people in a broken world. They fear burnout. They want to be great at what they do. They want to succeed in what God has called them to do, and they ask for advice.

After all these years I haven't found a better answer to give them than to desperately cling to the critical node of communicating directly with the Creator of the universe each day through His divinely inspired Word.

Sometimes I wish I had a more cool, modern, quotable response. But that is all I've got. It is simple, and I believe it is enough.

Focus on the simple critical node. Connect to the center of gravity. Go on offense. Value the volunteer.

It all sounded good. But would it actually work? There was only one way to find out.

Samurai

It was finally the night of the first Fields of Faith event. We had put together a leadership team made up of church youth leaders, coaches, teachers, and campus organizations who had a pulse on what God was doing through the youth on the campuses in the region.

Our planning meetings in the months leading up to the event had been a glimpse of heaven. Team members committed to unite and move all of their regularly scheduled church youth activities on Wednesday night to the local football field. That, in and of itself, was a miracle.

Unfortunately, churches across multiple denominations rarely worked together. But there was something about an event that featured their students facing an elevated challenge which placed them at the mic in front of their peers. It was bold and unique, which released an uncommon desire for bold and unique unity.

Our community was not the only one participating. Seventeen other Fields of Faith rallies were scheduled across Oklahoma, Kansas, and Texas. I still had no idea if this new strategy would even work.

We prayerfully sought the Lord to identify the right youth to put in front of their peers. The marketing was simple: students would invite their friends to come to an event at the local football field to hear their peers talk about their faith. That was it. No celebrity guest speakers. No pizza. No gimmicks. The students had to pull it off, or it would fail.

The adult leaders coached the student testimonies, organized the audiovisual technology, and prayed for clear weather. Our hopes were high.

Then the day of the event arrived, and the local weather map revealed the pending arrival of a massive deluge of rain across the region. It was as if God had planned for the heavens to release all of the water from Noah's flood onto the football stadium in Lawton, Oklahoma, on that Wednesday night. We hastily moved the sound system indoors to the gym before it got wet, but our hopes of anyone showing up to our event sank as fast as the waters rose. As I looked out over the empty gym, I thought to myself, *Well, it was a good idea. Time to move on to the next thing.*

But something strange began to happen. People started to show up.

They began to trickle in at first. The trickle became a stream, and it eventually seemed like a flood was happening inside the gym—but this flood was of people. I couldn't believe my eyes. School buses, cars, and church vans began to cover the parking lot. Before long, one side of the gym was full, and people were forced to sit on the gym floor. More than a thousand students from campuses and churches in Lawton and the surrounding communities had gathered together in the small college gym on that stormy night.

I immediately went into event management mode, making sure the audiovisual system was ready and the volunteers were in place to pull off an excellent program. You could feel the excitement caused by the unique unity everyone felt gathering for a common cause that was owned by everybody.

That excitement was about to come to a screeching halt for me. It suddenly hit me that I was about to find out if the earlier prognosticators were right about the folly of putting teenagers in front of their peers as the main speakers, especially in a reverberating gym with more than a thousand potentially bored and hyper students. There was a flurry of activity to get the program started with some initial announcements and some great music from a local youth band. Before I knew it, everything settled down to a quiet anticipation and the first speaker was at the microphone.

As I turned my head toward the empty, isolated microphone stand, I saw a petite young girl with a ponytail topped by a cute bow walk quietly up to the mic stand. I remember thinking how small and vulnerable she looked as I looked at the large, intimidating crowd that silhouetted her slight frame. *It's over*, I thought. It just seemed too overwhelming.

The crowd would rapidly digress into an unruly, bored mass of humanity that craved entertainment. This craving would lead to disrespect of the speaker, noisy interaction, and embarrassment for the student speakers and all the adults who made the mistake of giving them the mic. I would be responsible for destroying this young girl's confidence. She would probably never speak in public again.

It was my momentary slide into despair.

Then she gently reached into her pocket, pulled an item out, and began to speak.

"If I wanted to get into a fight, I could use this." She held up the item she had pulled out of her pocket. It was a small, pocketknife. She extended the short blade and poked it forward with several quick jabs.

She paused to let the crowd process what she had said.

"But if I got into a fight, I would rather use this." She slowly bent down and picked up something on the floor that she had placed by one of the audio speaker stands before she went up to the microphone. I had to look twice and blink my eyes to verify what I thought I saw.

It was a samurai sword.

She crisply pulled the sword out of its sheath and began a sweeping routine demonstrating her mastery of the sword. What followed was a series of swirling movements that had the grace and athleticism of a ballerina yet with a deadly sword arcing through the air in a coordinated flow of motion that took your breath away. I had no idea that she was a highly accomplished martial arts competitor. She ended her routine with a swift, precision movement of the sword from behind her head to the front of her body, the muscles of her arms tightened and fully extended with the tip of the sword pointing straight out in front of her. She let out a sharp, commanding "Hiyahhh!" and held that pose for what seemed like an eternity.

She then reached down and picked up a Bible from the floor in front of her. She looked directly out to the large crowd and said, "The Bible tells us that we need to put on the full armor of God. The only offensive weapon it mentions is the Bible, which is the sword of the Spirit. So I want to know how to properly use it, which is why I spend time in the Bible every day to know how to live my life." She paused to put her Bible down and pull out the small knife in one hand and hold the sword in the other. She stared intensely back at the crowd and said something I will never forget: "I don't want to use God's Word like this." She held up the pocket knife. "I want to use God's Word like this," and she held up the Samurai sword over her head. "I think you should join me and do the same."

"Thank you."

You could have heard a pin drop in the gym. Everyone was mesmerized by the piercing truth that was just shared by one of their own. It was one of those ministry moments where time seemed to stand still. All of the fears and doubts I had been battling were crushed by an all-powerful God as He had just used that young girl for His purpose in that moment.

A huge applause erupted from her peers. It didn't stop there. The next student got up. He shared what he had been learning from God's Word. He was anxious and stammered a bit with his words as he shared his heart. The next girl shared her biblical truth wrapped in nervous laughter and chasing thoughts as if she was herding cats. She went way too long. None of them were the polished speakers their generation had been raised to expect at every religious event.

But something became glaringly obvious as they shared. The crowd was locked in on every word they said, not because they were being entertained but because they could see themselves in the speakers. They identified with them.

The vast majority of people were not gifted at speaking in front of a crowd, small or big, but the stories they shared about struggling with chemistry homework, parents going through a divorce, or dealing with an injury in sports all hit home. These weren't stories from a celebrity with a life they would probably never have. This wasn't a gifted, elite ministry expert saying "be like me," which made the majority of people feel useless since they knew they couldn't conjure up someone else's gift with a wave of a hand. But they actually could be like those they were seeing and hearing on that night. They could read God's Word to find truth and try to be like Christ as best as they could each day.

We had decided to have an adult at the end of the program to wrap it up and give an invitation to respond. The adult was not the main part of the program, just someone to capture what the students said and sum it up. I was chosen by the leadership team to be that person. I simply got up and mentioned that their peers had done an amazing job of challenging them to read the Word of God and accept Jesus Christ as their personal Lord and Savior if they had never done that before. I invited them to come down to the gym floor if they wanted to talk about any faith decision they had been led to act on. I prayed a short prayer, and something amazing happened. A large number of the crowd immediately wanted to talk with someone. They came down so fast from the stands that there was a bottleneck at the rails located at the bottom of the steps that separated the stands from the gym floor. They started coming over the rails!

As our ministry team scrambled to make sure every student had someone to talk to, my cell phone started buzzing. One of the calls was from Midland, Texas. The excited voice on the other end was Eric Boyt, a passionate volunteer who took a chance on the students at Midland Lee High School and helped put together their Fields of Faith event. He shared that they had more than twenty-five hundred students show up at the Midland Lee High School football stadium. Midland Lee had gained national notoriety after the release of the hit movie *Friday Night Lights*. The same thing happened there as it had in Lawton. They had hundreds respond to an invitation, and they came over the rails onto the field. The ministry team was not prepared for such a response and adjusted by using the entire field as a counseling area.

Other rallies shared the same thing. Gatherings great and small had captured the imagination of the students as well as adults in attendance. One parent had dropped off her student at a stadium and stayed in the parking lot in their car during the program. She heard the testimonies of the students over the stadium loudspeaker. When the program was over, she stopped a pastor in the parking lot and prayed to receive Christ.

I was stunned at what had just happened on that rainy October night. The ordinary had taken the crowd to the critical node of Scripture. It had been so natural. So simple. They had risen from spectators in the crowd to heroes of the faith not because of their ability but because of their authenticity. They were the long tail, and they had been valued for that one night. They were ordinary, which brought attention to their God who is extraordinary. A small girl with a sword had helped birth a new movement that would soon spread across a nation. It was as simple as that.

Back to the Future

Fast-forward to October 2019. Now more than five hundred stadiums in more than forty states host Fields of Faith events of all sizes. More than a quarter of a million students gather at the stadiums.

The spiritual, cultural, and political landscape has changed dramatically. The country is much more polarized. Within this divisive and chaotic setting, a one-day, faith-based gathering of 250,000 students captures the attention of the national media.

Over the years I began to receive an ever-increasing list of requests from local, regional, and major national media outlets for interviews about Fields of Faith. I accepted many of the invitations at first but soon became wary when my words would sometimes be used out of context in some of the media outlets across the nation. You may be clear on your responses about a movement, but the media always has the last word on how they will construct their story to fit their predetermined narrative.

FCA partners with a communications firm that handles all media requests. During the week of Fields of Faith in October 2019, we were contacted by the highest rated news show on cable network TV, *Fox & Friends*.

Fox & Friends wanted to do a live interview on the program with a student discussing Fields of Faith! This was an unprecedented opportunity for FCA and for Fields of Faith. It presented a challenge, however. Fields of Faith was held on Wednesday, October 9. Fox wanted to do the live interview on Thursday morning, October 10, in their home studios located in downtown New York City.

I was faced with two barriers. One, I didn't really trust the media, since they seemed to have an affinity for taking any interview and twisting it into a political story. Two, while Fields of Faith had events in a majority of the states in the U.S., the largest and most impactful were in the South and Midwest parts of the country. If it were up to me, I would find one of the students from the larger Fields of Faith events in those locations who came from the Bible Belt, was a proven speaker, and who clearly understood the purpose of Fields of Faith while having experience talking in front of a camera, like a Division 1 college athlete who had done nationally televised interviews before.

This option was not on the table.

In New York, we only had two Fields of Faith events. I was shocked that we even had that many. One of those was being held at Hofstra University in New York City, and it was their first attempt at hosting the event.

I had never heard of Hofstra University. It is located on Long Island, which has a population of more than 7.5 million people. FCA had a grand total of one staff on Long Island. His name was Jason Harewood. Jason said it was hard to penetrate Hofstra University with any campus ministry presence. There had been limited ministry happening with none to the coaches and athletes until a coach named Justin Bentivegna and his wife, Jennifer, had arrived on campus two years previously. They started a small FCA huddle in their first year with a few athletes from the baseball and women's lacrosse teams. At the start of their second year, Coach Bentivegna and a few of the student leaders wanted to get more people involved and take their huddle to the next level. After talking with Jason Harewood and Frank Reynoso, one of our other FCA staff in New York, they decided to give Fields of Faith a shot. No one had ever done one, and most had never even heard of it, but they went ahead and reserved the softball stadium and hoped for good weather.

This scenario was far removed from another Fields of Faith event held on a different college campus located in West Texas at Texas Tech University. Over the course of three years, it had grown into the largest Fields of Faith event in the country. Attendance had steadily climbed to more than ten thousand in attendance, which included more than five hundred volunteers and sixty churches uniting from different denominations. Buses and vans from across West Texas would caravan from hundreds of miles away.

We only had one option for an interview with just a few hours to respond, and that option resided far away from the Bible Belt and somewhere among the millions of people in New York City. This was indeed an elevated challenge against all odds.

I was thankful and filled with dread at the same time. I was thankful that we had a potential option for the interview on such a massive stage. I was filled with dread because that someone was totally beyond my reach and control. I thought of all the work and sacrifice that my wife, my family, our volunteers, and I, as well as the FCA staff across the country, had put in over the past sixteen years to start and grow Fields of Faith. The top news show in the country was not just going to mention Fields of Faith; they were committing valuable airtime to an interview. Do you know how many businesses and organizations would kill for that type of free national coverage? All of that work would be represented by some unknown student from New York who would be the face and voice of Fields of Faith early the next morning. I had no idea what that person would say. I didn't know if they even really understood what Fields of Faith was all about. What if they froze up in front of the camera? What if they rambled on about things that didn't matter? What if the host asked questions in order to trap them into saying something politically controversial?

By the way, I didn't mention that my son AJ was getting married the next day and I was officiating the wedding.

I was a little anxious.

Everything was happening so fast. I texted some people that evening to be praying for the unknown student. My mom was one of those people. She had been at the first Fields of Faith event years earlier. As we texted back and forth, we both came to the same conclusion. I was having the same faith struggle I had leading up to the first event sixteen years ago.

There was an elevated risk in putting an ordinary student on the platform and giving him the microphone. There was an elevated challenge for the student to step up on such a large stage and speak boldly about his faith. I had little control. Success or failure lay squarely on the back of an ordinary student. I felt like I did at that college gym years before, watching a young girl walk up to the mic in front of a gym filled with her peers and thinking, *What have I done?*

> God delights in using the untrained, ordinary people to bring Him glory.

As I remembered back to that pivotal moment of doubt, I felt God gently reminding me that He had provided a special student back then, and He could do it again. He could provide another "Samurai" testimony. God delights in using the untrained, ordinary person to bring Him glory. We had seen Him do it. This was His event, His person, and His plan. New York City belonged to Him. He was in total control, and my faith needed to rest on that truth, not on my control.

I felt really stupid finding myself in the same crisis of doubt about the same situation (although on a much bigger stage!) that I had many years ago. But I confessed it to the Lord, and He was faithful and just to forgive me as He has always done. I was then able to go to sleep and rest without having any idea what would happen in the morning. That in itself was a miracle.

When I woke up the next morning, I shuffled into the kitchen to get a hot cup of coffee as I did every morning. My wife's best friend, Kare, and her husband, Stony, had come up from Austin, Texas, to Kansas City for my son's wedding and were staying with us. We all gathered in the living room, positioned ourselves comfortably on the couch, and eagerly turned on the TV.

It was somewhat surreal, since Julie watched *Fox & Friends* on that TV every morning as part of her routine getting ready for work. Here we were preparing to watch the same show that was going to feature something that had started out as a vision for us when no one else was watching and was now on a stage with the nation watching.

The segment finally came on after a commercial break. It started with a quick narrative overview of Fields of Faith featuring pictures from across the country of the stadium events that had just been held. The camera then panned across the stage featuring two chairs facing each other. One was for the host, Ainsley Earhardt, and the other was for our unknown student, who now became known to everyone.

Her name was Julianna Braniecki, a member of the Hofstra lacrosse team and part of the FCA huddle on campus. Her smile was absolutely contagious. She was beaming with joy. When the interview started, she was totally at ease. She answered every question with confidence as if she were having a conversation over coffee with Ainsley at the local Starbucks.

Ainsley, for her part, set the stage perfectly right out of the gates. She smiled at Julianna and said, "I love this organization. God used it to change my life when I was in college at the University of South Carolina."

The rest of the interview could not have been better if it were scripted. Julianna did a masterful job of communicating her faith and representing what Fields of Faith is all about. She was a positive, encouraging force on that national stage. When the four-minute interview was complete, we were in awe at how amazing the segment was. There were no trick questions or awkward moments. It was just an ordinary, authentic student talking about what Jesus had done in her life and sharing about an event that gave her a chance to talk about her faith.

Jason later shared that Julianna, a.k.a. "JuJu," was the only one of the four-member huddle leadership team who even had an opening in her schedule to do the interview at such a late date. She was also the least known by the FCA staff who had interacted with the huddle over the previous year. The first time they had even heard her share her testimony was at the Fields of Faith the night before.

Jason went on to share the challenges he had to face the day of their Fields of Faith event. They had been praying for great weather after reserving the softball stadium for their event. Sure enough, when the day arrived, the weather turned to rain and a temperature of 30 degrees along with windy conditions. Jason nervously awaited the decision from Hofstra FCA to move everything to a covered pavilion at the Lacrosse field. As part of the move, they were trying to get the word out to people about the last-minute change in location. He wasn't sure people who didn't live on campus and were planning to attend would be able to find the new location. During this flurry of adjustments being made on that rainy, cold afternoon, he received the communication about trying to help secure a student for the

Fox interview. Fox said they could have a car there to pick up the student at 5:00 a.m. the next morning.

Jason's first thought was, *Really? Of all the times for a request like this, it comes now?* But he contacted Coach Bentivegna, who immediately went to work contacting their leadership team members. The original goal was to secure two students so they could encourage and play off of each other in the interview. That plan evaporated quickly. Each student athlete he contacted couldn't do it due to morning class and workout schedules they couldn't miss. There would also need to be a release from the college compliance office, which they were able to get later in the afternoon. It all came down to JuJu, who said she could do it.

She had been a three-year member of the lacrosse team but rarely saw playing time due to a string of injuries that had sidelined her every season. She literally was the only one available in all of New York City who could meet the requirements for the interview, and she would now be doing the interview alone. After all, this is what ordinary heroes do. When given the opportunity, they walk into adversity against all odds.

When I talked with Jason about his experience, he indicated that he had to face some fear and doubt leading up to the interview. He didn't know how many students would show up to their Fields of Faith event due to the bad weather, and he didn't really know the student who would be sharing on the national stage. He had little control over what was happening. I shared with him that his experience was a mirror image of the feelings I had to wrestle with leading up to the first Fields of Faith event held sixteen years ago. The similarities were stunning.

Leaders are always seeking to do ministry and to get people to join us in what we are doing, but the influence of ordinary volunteers often travels much further. There is a boomerang effect on leaders when the volunteers begin to own their part of an epic story. I believe the greatest effect on the leader is a reminder of how much God is in control and we aren't. Jason shared that leading up to the Fields of Faith event, he had been at a critical crossroad with his participation in ministry. Things were going okay but nowhere near where he thought they would be. He questioned whether he was adding any value. Was there anything happening that was kingdom worthy? Was he making any dent for Jesus in the vast concrete jungle of New York City?

He said the event was perfect timing for him personally. It showed him that this was God's ministry, that he didn't have to force it. He said he was reminded that "God was running it and I'm allowed to be a part of it."

The next night at the wedding reception, one of my son's friends from Richmond, Virginia, shared with me that her dad, who lived in New York City, had forwarded the story and interview from the Fox website for her to watch that afternoon. He mentioned how encouraging it was to see a young college student in New York City being so bold with her faith. The segment was shared over and over through social media across the country.

Influence spreads quickly, and we have no control of where it flows.

Movement always happens when the ordinary is shown value and given a simple yet challenging task. Harewood shared that attendance at the Hofstra FCA huddle had increased significantly since the Fields of Faith event and the Fox interview. Athletes from most of the major sports on campus were now attending. He stated that the increased attendance hadn't been primarily a result of the interview but of a new boldness in the huddle members about their faith and inviting people to attend.

JuJu mentioned that the depth of the huddle increased. People really connected, including the existing huddle members. People came who had never heard anyone talk about the Bible. They could now hear about it. Their influence spread outside of their FCA huddle. The culture changed. She said it was no longer strange to invite people to the huddle. It was now culturally acceptable on campus to be invited to a faith group. They have started to serve in the community by volunteering with a church that recently

> Movement always happens when the ordinary is shown value and given a simple yet challenging task.

hosted a Tim Tebow sponsored event. The huddle at the U.S. Merchant Marine Academy at Kings Point had several of their leaders graduate the previous year and had not been able to identify new leadership to step into the void. The Hofstra huddle stepped into that void to help get the huddle up and running again. They are now helping plant ministries on other collegiate campuses.

It didn't stop there. JuJu, Coach Bentivegna, and his wife were invited to attend a major FCA donor event for the Northeast region of the U.S. They were able to share their story as one of several featured ministry specials in the program over the weekend. Those in attendance were moved by an incredible weekend of testimonies and fellowship. The weekend resulted in a 49-percent increase in giving over the previous two-year giving period from the same donors.

A student was trusted. She was shown value when she was given an opportunity to represent her faith, a ministry, and an event on a national stage. The message was simple. So simple that she could talk about it with confidence in front of millions with only hours to prepare. This never would have happened if the foundation of the Fields of Faith movement had been complex and hard to follow. One Day—One Message—One Stand.

RECAP

People who engage in reading the Bible at least four times a week experience profound effects on their lives. Anyone can do this. It is simple but powerful.

When the Word of God is made available in the language of the ordinary masses of people, spiritual awakening can happen.

A small girl with a sword and a simple message can spark a movement.

PART 4

COMMONALITY

If you chase two rabbits, you will lose them both.

NATIVE AMERICAN SAYING

CHAPTER 9

BIRDS OF A FEATHER

Team

I've talked to countless teams at all levels about this subject. Whether it was the Denver Broncos, the Oklahoma Sooner football team, or the Cache Pee Wee Football team, the desire was the same—teamwork. Teams and organizations are obsessed with this subject, and they should be. Humans universally seem to agree that teamwork is of vital importance, but consistently achieving it can be like trying to grasp oil in your hand.

Many organizations approach the challenge of creating teamwork like ski resorts just before the season begins. They spray artificial snow on the slopes in the weeks approaching the official opening to try to provide a layer of snow to guarantee at least some semblance of an opportunity to ski.

Whether it's pithy teamwork posters duct-taped to the wall, or a special guest speaker to come in and fire up the troops, leaders spray an artificial layer of motivation over the organization to provide a facade of teamwork, even though it's not the real thing.

One of the reasons it can be so difficult is that many variables are needed for it to actually happen. You are dealing with human beings—the most complex, unpredictable creatures on the planet. Organizational culture, societal and economic factors, as well as countless emotional and relational interactions can shift in the blink of an eye. This fact assures that teamwork cannot easily be manufactured or contained into a formula. But I believe some key guiding principles exist that can create the opportunity for teamwork to take root and eventually flourish with any group of people.

One of those principles became a bedrock to the successful launch of Fields of Faith.

The Principle of Seven

I had the opportunity at a conference with select, high-level global organizational leaders to sit next to an author named Lucas Ramirez, who wrote a fascinating book called *Designed for More: Unleashing Christ's Vision for Unity in a Deeply Divided World*.[1] He later gave a compelling presentation that captivated the audience. His talk captured my attention because it drilled

---

[1] Lucas Ramirez, *Designed for More: Unleashing Christ's Vision for Unity in a Deeply Divided World* (Nashville: FaithWords, 2018).

into one of the keys I had discovered of motivating people to start and expand a movement. It was foundational in what I had experienced at the genesis of the Fields of Faith movement.

I knew it was important. It had been a rally point which served as a magnet that attracted the collective desires and passions of the original team we had formed, who gathered around a big idea that could make a big difference.

What was it? Well, one of the best ways to understand it is to understand the subject of Ramirez's talk. The common starling.

A small bird found primarily in Europe, with large concentrations in England, the starling is about eight inches long and weighs about three ounces. It has a glossy, black iridescent plumage with a metallic sheen, which is speckled with white at different times of the year. The legs are pink, and the bill is black in winter and yellow in summer.

At first, I didn't understand where he was going with his talk. The room was filled with high-level global ministry leaders, and we were now talking about birds? But it didn't take long for him to reveal a principal that is essential to moving ordinary people from scattered involvement in a program or initiative to a passionate, almost desperate focus and drive to achieve something epic together.

You may have seen starlings flying through the air and not even known it. They form into a dazzling, undulating cloud that wildly swirls and arcs through the sky in one fluid motion. The phenomenon is called a murmuration. Hundreds and sometimes thousands of starlings form a flock marked by pinpoint changes in direction and speed with almost instant synchronization.

It is art in motion that can captivate and mesmerize humans anchored to a more predictable, stable surface of dirt and rock.

Many studies in collective animal behavior focus on trying to understand how enterprise-level order can emerge from such simple behavioral rules.

Scientists using advanced video analysis tools and computational modeling reveal that their patterns are known less from biology and more from cutting-edge physics. Their best description of the uncanny synchronization found in a starling murmuration is "critical transitions," systems that are poised to tip, to be almost instantly and completely transformed. They have also described the phenomenon as "scale-free correlation." How this starts and maintains is what scientists can't figure out.

However, the movement rule of an individual starling is extremely simple. When your neighbor moves, so do you.

In fact, the science reveals great insight on how the interconnected movements happen. Research indicates that the holistic movement of the flock hinges on the movement between the individual starlings with those closest to them. It was determined that the movements are a result of distance and coordination of each starling with their nearest seven neighbors. Each starling has a reaction time of under one hundred milliseconds, illustrating just how quickly they can respond to another's flight pattern. This results in a dynamic system marked by individual parts combining to make a whole of collective synchronization, and a murmuration suddenly emerges in the sky.

While scientists and biologists have systematically closed in on how a murmuration works, one of the more pressing

questions was, *Why does a murmuration form in the first place?* Is it
some kind of mating ritual or elaborate bonding technique? The
answer to this question captured my attention and imagination.

It was a peregrine falcon.

A common enemy attacking the starlings is what causes their
seemingly spontaneous cohesion into a coordinated, pulsating
flock.

The primary motivator to unite is survival.

When a flock is under attack from a predator, the principal
of seven engages with lightning speed, optimizing team cohesion
with individual effort. The group responds in unison and can't
be dispersed into individual subgroups. It becomes an emergent,
living organism, which is never
led by a single individual. They
are governed collectively by all
of the flock members.

When one starling changes
direction or speed, each of
the other birds reacts to the
change with seamless agility. The information travels like a bolt
of lightning across the flock with practically no degradation.
This allows a starling on one side of the flock to react to what
the others are sensing all the way on the opposite side of the
flock, regardless of the size. This enlarges what researches call
the "effective perceptive range" of every starling, which greatly
enhances their ability to avoid a full-on strike from a diving
falcon.

Just imagine how incredibly difficult this makes it for the
falcon to focus on any one bird at a time. It is no longer diving

> **The primary
> motivator to unite is
> survival.**

in on an easy meal of one hapless, unaware starling. The falcon now must account for a highly coordinated flock that moves as one in response to the starlings closest to the falcon as it dives into the flock. The slightest motion change along the edge of the formation initiates a rapid collective evasive maneuver that instantly bursts across the flock. The principal of seven neighbors unleashes an agile, quick symmetry that leaves the falcon to attack and hit only air, missing all the starlings. As Ramirez puts it, "The more fierce the attack, the more beautiful the formation becomes."[2]

Unity was forged from the clear and present danger of a vicious predator with one goal, to kill the prey. The predator longs to see the flock scatter. In disorganized chaos the prey can be seen, targeted, and subdued. Success for the starlings is only possible with one goal—unity.

What a powerful truth for any organization! Yes, everyone will agree that unity is important, but seeing an organization operate as a cohesive, agile organism with each individual caring and coordinating with their closest seven neighbors is a rarity. In other words, acknowledging the importance of unity and actually unifying are two vastly different things. Ramirez says, "The starlings in a Murmuration never collide because they all have the same strategy built on relationships and awareness. It's crystal clear in their minds who the *real* enemy is. For the church, we are confused about which direction to fly in and which enemy to flee from, leaving us incapable of murmurating."[3]

---

[2] Ramirez, *Designed for More*, 96.
[3] Ramirez, *Designed for More*, 99.

It struck me how the idea of commonality can drive to cohesion: a common goal, a common belief, a common interest, etc. But a common enemy? There is something more visceral that quickly prioritizes and clarifies what is important when your people are facing something that doesn't care about your various beliefs, interests, squabbles, and differences. If something or someone has a goal to annihilate something you and others hold dear, you have a common enemy that can cause one collective heartbeat where previously there were many. People start to pay attention and care about those in their immediate surroundings. Almost everyone has connections with at least seven people around them. What if all your volunteers or employees in your organization began to pay acute attention and serve their seven closest neighbors? What if those groups of seven naturally connected with other groups of seven? What if the groups of seven continued to expand rapidly? That is what a common enemy can do. It can start a murmuration within your organization that spreads into the public and requires no central leader but depends on ordinary people leveraging their influence on those around them. That is the power of the principle of seven.

Becoming One

The small room was located in the corner of the church. Lots of meetings are held in churches. I had attended and led more than I could remember. But this one was different.

I had invited the people in the room because they had been identified as youth leaders who had their fingers on the spiritual pulse of their communities. We had been in the ministry trenches together over the years. We knew and trusted one another. In the room were youth pastors and leaders from various denominations and youth organizations, teachers and coaches from different schools, and businesspeople. The meeting wasn't called with the primary purpose of pitching a new program or resource or to network. There was a seriousness in the air.

I began the meeting sharing about the sincere frustration I felt, almost a desperation about how the culture had become increasingly hostile and aggressive toward the sincerely held beliefs of the followers of Jesus. I painted the picture of how I felt that families were being surrounded in a 360-degree spiritual fight, always on defense. Scattered. Chaotic.

I made clear what I thought needed to be said: "We are losing."

I believed we had to acknowledge that we were in a fight for survival, and the enemy wasn't a political party, the music industry, Hollywood, the media, activists that seemed to march and protest with increasing boldness, or a multitude of other things that arose every day. We were all trying to defend against all of them all of the time. It was exhausting.

The room got solemn as I painted a grim picture of what I felt we were facing. I was convinced it was imperative we agreed that we were losing. I also felt we couldn't move forward until we peered into the darkness to clearly identify who was behind it all.

It was Satan. The ancient adversary of God. I quoted the description from the Bible: "He is 'like a roaring lion, looking for anyone he can devour'" (1 Pet. 5:8). "He seeks 'to steal and kill and destroy'" (John 10:10). He waits at the doorway of my house so he can have me (Rev. 3:20).

He was it. He was our common enemy. He was the predator diving into and scattering the flock.

In fact, another name for Satan found in Scripture is the devil or *diabolos*, which means "scatterer."

The Bible begins with an opening scene featuring God creating everything, resulting in perfect unity and harmony in the garden of Eden. God walked with Adam and Eve in the garden. All animals and the environment lived in perpetual unison and peace. This was the original intent for all creation. Within a millisecond of the decision to take the fruit from the tree of the knowledge of good and evil, the original intent was destroyed. A tectonic rift formed in the relationship between mankind and God. The harmony of the earth and its inhabitants was broken. In essence, all creation became scattered.

The closing scene in the Scripture indicates that the original intent of the creation will be realized. All things will be made new. There will be a new heaven and a new earth. Everything that has been scattered will be joined together once again.

In the meantime, mankind plays out all the other scenes in this epic story. There resides in the heart of every person the original longing for unity with God, one another, and the environment. It has been there from the beginning and possesses a deep, untapped power that is unleashed when the proper conditions emerge to release it. Those conditions can be difficult to create. Many times they are right under our noses. They are so simple that we miss them.

I then saw something incredible start to happen at that moment.

Church youth programs in our area hosted some of their most important outreach meetings of the week on Wednesday nights. Most of the school extracurricular activities and sports events would not schedule their activities on Wednesday nights to allow students and their families to attend midweek church services. This was a highly coveted time slot for churches to consistently meet with and minister to their youth groups. Most churches would plan their big youth programs for Wednesday night; it was almost considered a teenager holy day in the South.

It was a bold question, but I asked the youth pastors to consider the idea of moving their regularly scheduled ministry activities to the local stadium. I wasn't asking them to cancel their youth programs, just move them to a different place and join other church youth programs from all the denominations and organizations in the area.

I had no idea if they would think that was a good idea or if they would treat me as a heretic and ask me to leave the meeting and never come back! I knew some of them would be frowned upon for even mentioning the idea to their pastors. The status quo never likes to lose status or quo. The room got awkwardly quiet as everyone looked around at one another, wondering if anyone would offer their program up as a sacrifice to a risky idea.

Suddenly a voice came from my left, "We're in." It was Jamie Austin, the youth pastor of the largest church youth program in the city. In fact, they had just invested and built a large, expensive, cutting-edge modern building designed specifically for youth ministry. If there was any program I thought had the most to lose by moving their activities to a local football field on a Wednesday night, it was Jamie's. They didn't need to join together for a big event in town; they already were the big event in town.

Yet here was Jamie being the first one to come on board. "We're locking the doors and sending them to the stadium," he said. Once that happened, it was like a row of dominoes. All the other churches joined in. It was beautiful to watch. There is something awe-inspiring when people and organizations willingly delay their regularly scheduled activities, plans, and expectations in order to chase something bigger together.

I watched a murmuration form right in front of my eyes.

Everyone in the room saw the enemy. We knew we were losing our culture that valued faith in God. We could sense the predator. We saw the devastation Satan could do and was doing in our community. Suddenly we began to move as one, just like the starlings. Everyone was no longer thinking about their own program the same way as when they had entered into that room earlier in the day.

> **People don't just want to take *in* something; they want to take *on* something.**

Once we all saw the predator, we began to fly in a new, synchronized pattern. We closed ranks and had a desire to coordinate our movements. The conversation shifted from what each of our own programs was doing to how we could unite our individual programs into one powerful event. It wasn't going to be easy, but the high challenge we had accepted brought a new energy and excitement to the room. We were different when we walked out of that room. We went in as individuals; we came out as a team.

We had been birds flying different directions; we were now different birds flying in the same direction. We began to move in a highly coordinated pattern interacting with our closest neighbors, which gave us a chance against the attacks of our common enemy.

Remember, people don't just want to take *in* something; they want to take *on* something.

RECAP

A common enemy will mobilize a common response.

A clearly defined predator can cause people to stop thinking about themselves and their programs and think more about those closest around them. The principle of seven.

People don't just want to take in something; they want to take on something.

CHAPTER 10

IDENTIFY YOUR ENEMY

Define It

What is your common enemy?

Is your organization made up of people or departments just flying around in the air? They may be flying in the same general direction, but are they highly coordinated with a desire to care, read, and respond to those closest to them in order to survive?

Common goals are needed in order to plan tasks that help you achieve the goals you set. These are critical to achieving anything. While goals and metrics can be great motivators, they rarely release the deep part of the human spirit driven by an insatiable desire to survive. A common enemy awakens that desire that for many people gets buried in the mundane rhythm and responsibilities of work, family, and life.

All of the great stories have two key components, the hero and the villain. The villain is someone or something that seeks to bring harm to the hero and many times seems to be invincible. How is the hero possibly going to overcome the villain and win the day?

What is the villain of your organization? Instead of thinking about what goals you want to achieve, what about a common enemy you want to defeat? This is possible in every business or organization.

This isn't about coming up with a common enemy within your organization. It isn't about addressing complaints of needs not being met. While these need to be constantly assessed and addressed, doing so won't spark a movement. The great businesses don't see their organization as the hero; they see their customers as the hero. They obsess over how their organization can help their customers overcome a common enemy and be the hero of the story.

I was discussing this idea with a president of the board of trustees of a ballet company. He mentioned that their board hosted several large annual fundraisers with a goal of securing donations to underwrite their operational budget each year in their city. Paying the bills and maintaining programs is critical to any organization. Setting and hitting these goals is of utmost importance. I asked the question of how defining a common enemy in addition to determining their common goals could affect their operations. If so, then what would be their common enemy?

He thought for a moment and suggested that they did a lot in the community to raise awareness for the arts. He felt it was important that a society have an appreciation of the arts in order to progress and succeed. I suggested that perhaps a common enemy for their organization would be an ignorance of the arts. Ignorance could eliminate what they had to offer and could damage the community, the city, and our society. Ignorance cared nothing for the goals of their ballet company; in fact, it wanted to eliminate them.

What if their stated common goal shifted from raising a specified amount of money at an event to defeating the common enemy of a rising ignorance of the arts in their community? What if the heroes were not the board of trustees and their fundraisers but the ballet dancers and the myriad of volunteers who made their community engagement programs happen throughout the year, affecting thousands of people? What if the board of trustees' sole purpose was to help the dancers and volunteers be the heroes of the story?

This shifted the conversation from operating exclusive high-level board activities to possibly including more of the volunteers and ballet dancers on some of the advisory committees to create deeper value and ownership. Clearly defining the challenge of a rising ignorance of the arts in the city would inject much-needed passion and purpose in the predictable and mundane annual performances and programs. Their existing community outreach programs could take on a new urgency. The funding events would be driven by a united desire to survive by defeating their common enemy of ignorance of the arts rapidly spreading across the city. Every dollar raised would not be for the purpose of "supporting a good cause" or to sponsor a fun event. It was much more serious. There would be high challenge with a lot on the line.

Our conversation had shifted from predictable organizational operations to inspiring, innovative thoughts and ideas.

Mart Green, chief strategy officer for Hobby Lobby, states this principle in this way: "I'm a part of a collaborative effort called Every Tribe Every Nation, which is a partnership between ministry partners and Gospel Patrons to 'Eradicate Bible Poverty.' We want to make sure all 7,000 people groups have access to Scripture in their heart language by 2033."[4]

He could have easily said, "Our goal is to get a Bible in the hands of seven thousand people groups by 2033." This would be a common goal that is measurable and has a time line. But he did it in a different way. He mentioned a common enemy they want to "eradicate," which is "Bible poverty." This is about uniting in order to bring down an enemy that is threatening millions of people. Same goal, different motivation. There is something visceral and urgent about a common enemy that can inspire and move people to action.

I wondered how many businesses and nonprofit organizations were missing out on this untapped unity that could easily be accessed by the simple step of defining a common enemy.

Proving Ground

I have been involved in sports ministry for more than twenty-five years. The thousands of coaches and athletes I have

---

[4] John Rinehart, *Gospel Patrons: People Whose Generosity Changed the World* (Scotts Valley, CA: CreateSpace Independent Publishing Platform, 2014).

worked with over the years are key igniters of the principle of commonality in their communities. Practically every community around the world naturally unites around their local sports teams.

An opponent is coming to town with a stated goal of defeating your team, your people, your colors, your traditions. In no way is a sports team an enemy, but it is an opponent that wants to claim victory over your team. Your local team has set individual and team goals throughout the year to get bigger, stronger, faster, and more technically sound in their skill sets. But those common individual and team goals are not what unleashes a fan murmuration. The principle of a common enemy ignites a once dispersed population into a collective living organism that fills a stadium to support their team. Something deep in the soul of mankind wants to unite and overcome.

Examples of unity in the community are easy to spot when it comes to sports. Grown men will pay a large amount of their hard-earned money to purchase and don a jersey with another man's name stitched on the back. All kinds of people from every background, race, and socioeconomic status will purchase team shirts, flags, hats, pants, scarves, and every other apparel and promotional product known to man that bears the logo and colors of your team. If the team is really good, out comes the face and body paint, crazy wigs and masks. You name it, fans will wear it. They will passionately rally around and belt out a common fight song. They aggressively unite around team chants and cheers. Every time a big play occurs, they will erupt together in a cheer and turn to their closest neighbors in the stands for a celebratory high five. They may have never met the closest seven fans around them, but for a brief, shiny moment, they are part of a collective consciousness that moves together as one. The energy generated in those few hours is exhilarating.

I recently watched this play out in dramatic fashion where I live in Kansas City. My wife and I live in a downtown high-rise apartment in the Power and Light District, which is a vibrant entertainment area located in the heart of the city.

The Kansas City Chiefs made a dramatic run in the NFL playoffs, earning a berth in the Super Bowl, which is the largest single sports event in America, typically garnering more than 100 million viewers for the big game. Power and Light hosted a Super Bowl watch party in the Live Block that is surrounded by a wide variety of restaurants and sports bars. The space is first come, first served for concerts and large outdoor events held throughout the year. The game started at 5:30 p.m. People were lining up at 7:00 a.m. that morning to get into the Live Block area. By 9:00 a.m. it was full. Approximately twenty thousand attended. No seating, they all stood. The sea of fans dressed in red stayed not only to the end of the game at 9:00 p.m. but late into the morning after the Chiefs won the Super Bowl. They stood and chanted and danced and sang and cheered as one for more than nineteen hours. Believe me, I saw it from my balcony and heard the celebration late into the morning!

Three days later there was a champions parade and victory celebration. Fans bundled up and braved subfreezing temperatures as they lined the streets before dawn. Many of them spent the night in the frigid temperature to secure their place on the lawn where the parade ended, and a massive victory celebration was to be held. More than 800,000 fans high-fived, waved pennants, performed what seemed to be a perpetual tomahawk chop chant, danced, took pictures, and scurried up trees and other structures to get a better view.

I thought of the difference in countries led by dictators that force the population to attend military parades and cheer for their glorious leader. They always get a crowd, but it is coerced.

The KC fans all attended on their own accord. They willingly volunteered to endure the highly elevated elements of discomfort in order to watch and celebrate their team defeating their common opponent in the biggest contest of the year. They wanted to unite and be part of something epic.

Is it any wonder that, as our society continues to fragment into millions of niches with compelling statistics indicating that this is one of the loneliest generations in history, sports have risen to historic prominence? Could it be that it is one of the last bastions that can unify a community and satisfy a deep desire to be part of an epic cause against a high challenge to overcome a common enemy?

RECAP

In addition to developing common goals, take time to identify a common enemy that your organization is facing. Unity will be the result.

Sports in a community is a great example of how a common opponent can unite a community.

PART 5

OWNERSHIP

Then I heard the voice of the Lord asking:
"Who will I send? Who will go for us?"
I said: "Here I am. Send me."

ISAIAH 6:8

CHAPTER 11

STAGE FRIGHT

Rent

There is a profound difference between signing a lease contract on an apartment and signing a contract to purchase your first home. Think about how you treat a rental car versus a shiny new car you just bought and drove off a car lot.

When you purchase a large item like a home or a car, it affects everything about you. Emotionally, you have feelings of joy, anticipation, and excitement. Physically your heart beats a little faster, your pulse picks up, and the muscles of your face form into ongoing smiles releasing endorphins into your bloodstream. Relationally you want to tell your friends all about your new purchase and post it on all your social media channels. It even affects you spiritually with a deep feeling of accomplishment that reinforces your sense of identity.

When you finally complete the purchase of a new car, you gently drive your new car off the lot with extra awareness of who and what is on the road all around you. You make sure no one smudges the console or seat cushions, and your righteous wrath will be released on anyone daring to leave any trash in your new car! You wash it and wax it on a consistent basis, whether it needs it or not. After all, it is *your* car.

Renting a car brings nowhere near the same response. You don't see a lot of people posting selfies proudly standing beside their recently rented midsize sedan. When it comes to driving your rented car, you don't give a second thought to accidently hitting a pothole because the shocks don't belong to you. You whip around corners without a care in the world for the extra tread wearing off the tires; after all, they're not your tires. You don't scan the parking lot for the best spot to make sure someone doesn't open their door and ding your car because you were a little too close to them at Walmart.

Both are cars. Totally different effects.

This is the power of ownership. It can release the best in us. It heightens our senses as we become more aware of our surroundings. Ownership can be an extension of who we are. We can feel the difference we are making. Our focus intensifies. Our desire to carry out our part to completion at all costs is insatiable. After all, it is my part!

When it comes to volunteers, people around them know if they are renters or owners.

Volunteers who are renters don't elicit that same visceral response. There's a connection to something important they need, to be of help, but it normally ends there. The values and goals of the organization aren't actually theirs. They are borrowing them for a designated period of time before they turn them back in. After all, it is much easier to use it and drop it off when you're done. The organization gets something positive and so does the volunteer, but this is nowhere near the power of ownership.

An old saying holds true here: when it comes to a breakfast of eggs and bacon, the chicken is involved, but the pig is all in!

Renters have never started a movement; owners are the ones who spark movement. The question each organization needs to ask, then, is if your strategy is to build your organization to seek renters or owners. You will get what you advertise for.

Learn to Fly

In July 2015, a young man named Fabio Zaffagnini in the small town of Cesena, Italy, came up with a big idea. Fabio was a huge fan of the American rock band Foo Fighters. He wanted to get the multiple Grammy award-winning band to come to his town to perform a live concert. Foo Fighters had performed around the world for many years. Their popularity was global. One of their concert stops at Wembley Stadium sold out the eighty-six thousand seats not once or twice but three nights in a row. That's 258,000 people in three nights! Some of their concerts were almost as big as the entire population of Cesena which contained fewer than 100,000 people.

The magnitude of Fabio's idea was laughable, and that is exactly what everyone did when he started talking to them about it. But that didn't stop him from acting on his idea.

He came up with a plan to find one thousand volunteer musicians who would gather together in one place and get them to simultaneously play a Foo Fighters song, resulting in the biggest rock show ever. They would capture the performance on video and send it, along with a plea to perform a concert in Cesena, to Dave Grohl, the lead singer of Foo Fighters.

He began to put the word out and gather the volunteers it would take to pull it off. He had no idea if he could even find that many, but some local musicians began to sign up. The idea jumped from the local area and they began to attract others to sign up from across Italy and other countries. The musicians came from every walk of life. For the most part they weren't professionals—although world-renowned composer Marco Sabiu did volunteer to conduct the performance. The volunteers simply loved music and could play an instrument or sing as a hobby or side gig. Each one went through a screening process and, most importantly, were like-minded in this vision. They consisted of guitar players, bass players, drummers, and singers. All were tasked with memorizing the 1999 Foo Fighters hit, "Learn to Fly." They would have to cover their own expenses to get to the performance.

The performers were volunteers, but money was needed to pull off this ambitious goal. Sound systems, marketing, administration, etc., had to be covered, so they started a crowd-funding campaign to raise enough funds to cover the costs of the event.

They somehow gathered the needed funds and eventually all gathered in a park for the performance. The vision for the event had moved people.

The day of the event finally arrived in July, and the feeling was electric. The once empty field now contained a tapestry of symmetrical rows made up of eclectic performers clad in whatever apparel suited their individual style. They were arranged by instrument and voice groupings. A tall tower of scaffolding rose from one end of the field to provide a visible stage from which Marco Sabiu could direct the one song concert.

As the cameras rolled, a hush descended on the field as Sabiu strolled elegantly up to the edge of the platform. He cast his gaze out over the field of the expectant musicians. He raised his hands in a swooping arc then brought them down with quick precision, and the concert was on. The different instruments belted out their parts in amazing unison. The singers clustered around the mics sang with an intensity and joy that was contagious. Smiles covered the field.

These volunteer musicians immediately realized they were part of something incredible happening right in front of their eyes. They were not just doing their hobby or playing a side gig in front of a few disinterested people in a dark pub or hole-in-the-wall coffee shop. They weren't just attending a Foo Fighters concert and hearing "Learn to Fly" in a large crowd at Wembley Stadium. They *were* the concert! They were doing something that had never been done before. They had been given the microphone, and the cameras were focused on them collectively. They moved as one. Their synchronized passion was contagious, and it grew stronger as the song was played out.

When the song was completed, Fabio gave an impassioned plea directly into the camera for Foo Fighters to come to Cesena to perform: "Italy is a country where dreams cannot easily come true. But it's a land of passion and creativity. What we did here was a huge miracle," he said. "This is all that we got, 1,000 rockers that came from all over the nation at their own expenses. And they did for just one song . . . your song."[1]

The footage was captured and edited into a mesmerizing video that was sent to the band. It was also placed on YouTube and immediately went viral with more than fifty million views, a number that still grows to this day.

Five months later, on November 3, 2015, a unique live show was held in Cesena, Italy. Foo Fighters gave a three-hour concert dedicated to the Thousand, all the donors and volunteers that had made the July performance a reality.

The original big idea that had generated only laughter in the beginning now generated amazement and admiration from people around the world.

Fabio Zaffagnini had successfully created an opportunity for ordinary volunteers not just to be involved in a high challenge but to be the primary determiner of its success or failure. This high level of trust unleashed a radical personal and collective ownership of the vision. It was not about money. The musicians and singers received no compensation and even paid their own way to get to the event. They didn't just rise to the challenge; they obliterated it. Each volunteer knew they had to accomplish their individual part at a high level for the event to be a success. This is called ownership.

---

[1] Jeff Gorra, "The Legacy of the Rockin' 1000," Artist Waves, January 10, 2017, accessed September 23, 2020, http://artistwaves.com/the-legacy-of-the-rockin-1000.

Challenge Us!

High Challenge + High Trust = High Ownership

Low Challenge + Low Trust = Low Ownership

This is exactly what we experienced when we took a chance on teenagers being the featured speakers at our event. They all rose to the challenge. It took them out of their comfort zones. It wasn't easy for them. But it worked.

It was not uncommon for the featured teenagers giving testimonies to be extremely nervous and anxious in the moments leading up to their time at the mic in front of their peers. I remember one night being behind the stage with several of the teenagers preparing to share their testimonies. The event was being held on a field at a large college football stadium. One of them was a quarterback of a local football team that played its home games in the stadium hosting the event. In fact, he had just played in that stadium the previous Friday in front of ten thousand fans, leading his team to an exciting victory in a big rivalry game. The football game had featured local and statewide media, bright lights, and big-time pressure to perform. I assumed if anyone would have confidence speaking to about a thousand other teenagers, it would be this young man. But that was not the case. I noticed him pacing back and forth in the shadows. I approached him and asked him if he was doing okay. He shared that he had never been that nervous in his life. He said that he felt like he was getting ready to throw up! He was at a point of high challenge. He had to step up to that challenge.

I had raised the expectation for him. He wasn't expected to just sit in the crowd and listen; he was partially responsible for the success or failure of the event. I took all the scheduled student speakers into the locker room as the worship band played on the stage outside. I gently encouraged them not to try to be something they weren't. I let them know we didn't need them to suddenly become incredible communicators. We just needed them to be authentic and share their Bible story in their own way. They had everything they needed to make a difference.

I saw a calm confidence settle over them. We prayed together and went onto the field. One by one they stepped onto the stage and closed the distance to the microphone. They were amazing. They knew they were trusted to achieve something great. They overcame their fears and owned their part to accomplish something amazing together.

Periodically providing increased pressure can produce a new tapestry. Think of when you draw with a colored pencil or a crayon. You can glide the tip across the paper to draw a design and capture the color. But when you increase the pressure on the paper, a deeper, more brilliant hue emerges that immediately adds depth and beauty to the drawing. If you do this too often, you will need to sharpen the pencil, and you will run out of crayon to draw with. This is no different with volunteers. When you periodically create an environment of heightened expectation, it creates a deeper, more brilliant result from the heart of the volunteer. This can't be all the time, or you will burn them out. But when it is done at just the right time, the result can be a beautiful canvas.

RECAP

Renting and ownership are not the same. One is for temporary use, the other is an extension of who we are.

There is a profound difference between attending a concert and being the concert. When volunteers are the concert, ownership happens.

High Challenge + High Trust = High Ownership

Low Challenge + Low Trust = Low Ownership

CHAPTER 12

THE PACK

Get Over It

> Responsibility equals accountability equals ownership. And a sense of ownership is the most powerful weapon a team or organization can have. —Pat Summit

In such a distracted and disjointed society, it can be difficult to motivate volunteers to own their part in your organization. Because of this difficulty, we tend to lower the bar of expectation in order to at least get a small semblance of a win so we can feel good about ourselves as volunteers step or stumble over the low bar we have set for them.

The idea of rallying people to climb a seemingly impossible peak together fraught with obstacles, risk, and a high chance of failure is something that runs counter to our natural inclination to eliminate as much risk as possible as we plan, prepare, and control everything to achieve a predictable outcome.

But avoiding any high challenge whatsoever is a direct cause of our frustration with unmotivated or disinterested volunteers. We attempt to coddle or guilt them into being involved in easily achievable tasks. Now don't get me wrong—these smaller tasks are vital and important for any organization to maintain ongoing operations. But when this becomes the overwhelming majority of what you are asking of your volunteers, they will descend to that norm or look elsewhere to meet their deep need to be part of something epic. In the high challenge, the heart of the volunteer is moved, resulting in passionate ownership and incredible impact. Volunteers are waiting on someone or some organization to trust what they have to bring to the cause.

> In the high challenge, the heart of the volunteer is moved, resulting in passionate ownership and incredible impact.

Just like all great stories, the hero needs a high challenge to achieve and a villain doing everything possible to defeat them. No one talks about the hero who achieved a small, predictable goal with little to nothing on the line. Tapping into a volunteer who owns their part is similar to splitting the atom. You are working with something small and unseen, but within it resides great power that can change everything around it when the conditions exist to release it into the world.

If vision is the heart of a movement, ownership is the blood that pulses through its veins.

Judy

My grandfather was larger than life. He grew up on a farm in the hills of Arkansas. His life cast a large shadow. He was a big, athletic man, which earned him a football scholarship to the University of Oklahoma where he became an All-American. He earned one of the great sports nicknames of his time during his playing days as a Sooner: "Cactus Face." Upon graduation, he was drafted by the New York Giants and spent the next seven years playing professional football for the New York Giants, Chicago Cardinals, Pittsburgh Steelers, Buffalo Bills, and Los Angeles Dons, later to become the Rams.

During his time as a professional football player, his legend only grew. Duggan would be seen partying and playing poker with Joe DiMaggio when the Giants and Yankees were in town the same weekends in October. After being traded to the Los Angeles Dons, he became a regular at the elaborate parties held at the Hollywood mansions of team owners, which included Hollywood titan Louis Burt Mayer, who was a film producer and cofounder of Metro-Goldwyn-Mayer (MGM) studios. Other owners included actors/entertainers Bob Hope, Bing Crosby, and Academy Award winner Don Ameche.

As his professional football playing career wound down, Cactus Face became a member of the Oklahoma Highway Patrol. The legendary stories of his harrowing encounters and shootouts with criminals seemed to float between fact and fiction.

Upon retirement from the highway patrol, he started a successful heavy-equipment construction business. Large equipment moving large amounts of earth and other objects was a perfect fit for such a larger-than-life personality.

Cactus Face was considered a skilled "horse trader." This term figuratively describes someone who is adept at transacting or negotiating trades of any kind.

An endless supply of machinery, tools, vehicles, guns, and animals rotated through the Duggan property. He had a keen eye for horses and dogs and rarely brought one home without excellent, proven bloodlines.

His bird-hunting dogs were always from top breeders and were considered some of the most prolific in the region. The dogs worked the prairies and brush of Oklahoma with surgical precision. No anxious dove or cowering quail had a chance when his dogs were on point.

With all the revolving livestock and hunting dogs that would pass through, seeing a new animal on the property was commonplace, and we thought nothing of it.

One day I walked by the barn and saw a dog sitting in the shadows that was a little different from the other breeds I was accustomed to seeing. It looked nothing like the bird dogs and other hunting dogs I had seen. I knew it was a full-bred dog. I just couldn't identify what breed it was.

It stood out because it looked so normal. Even its name was normal: Judy.

It wasn't a talented bird dog.

It wasn't some huge sight-hunting dog bred exclusively to bring down large game.

There was nothing exotic about it. It was just . . . ordinary.

Judy had a short, dense coat of hair the color of wheat with a dark muzzle on her face. Her coat perfectly matched the color of the surrounding prairie grass common in the vast plains of the Midwest. The dog was slightly muscular, weighing approximately seventy pounds and standing about twenty-seven inches in height.

One thing that stood out was the hair along her spine. It ran the opposite direction of the rest of her hair. It looked as if someone had brushed the hair upwards forming something similar to a quasi-Mohawk running down her back.

The dog was always quiet. She never barked, and she continuously seemed to be scanning everything around her, acutely aware of all her surroundings.

I could never get close enough to Judy to pet her. Judy never tucked her tail and darted away. She never seemed afraid. She always kept a calculated distance from me with a wary eye on my every movement when I was near. She only allowed my granddad to put a hand on her, so I just basically left her alone. I didn't ask my grandfather what breed the dog was since I never interacted with it, basically out of sight, out of mind.

I soon noticed that Judy was beginning to gain weight. It became apparent that my grandfather had Judy bred and she was carrying a litter. It wasn't long before the litter of four brown pups appeared. I knew better than to go anywhere close to them. Every time I approached the area where the pups were tucked safely away in the back of the barn, I would get a threatening look from Judy accompanied by a low, controlled growl. I would stop in my tracks and back slowly away. There was something different about this dog. There was the sense of a primal, wild core wrapped in a domestic, controlled shell.

Over the coming months, the pups grew rapidly. They began to venture out and explore their surroundings under the watchful eye of their mother. Wherever she walked, they would follow with clumsy leaps and bounds as their agility attempted to catch up to their ever-growing frames.

As a young boy, I desperately wanted to play with the litter of pups. But I knew that would never happen as long as they were with Judy. So I left well enough alone and never chanced it.

My family was never as judicious in our selection of dogs. We did not approach the choice of dogs as my grandfather did. We were never interested in pure, champion bloodlines of hunting or working dogs. In fact, we were not interested in dogs at all. We rarely purchased a dog. Any dogs we had wandered up to us, not the other way around. Our dog was a small mutt named Sweetie.

We lived on five acres next to my grandparents' vast property. One day I grabbed my fishing pole and tackle box, whistled for Sweetie, and took off for my favorite pond, which contained more bass, crappie, and perch than the other ponds combined.

Sweetie always walked to my right, slightly ahead, almost like a scout. As we crossed an open field, I saw movement off in the distance in the knee-high prairie grass. A lot of grass was moving from something coming toward us. I soon noticed five brown tails protruding and weaving through the grass headed in our direction. It was Judy and her now adolescent pups, almost full-grown. I had seen them before in the distance as they moved effortlessly together across the open prairie and through the wooded game trails. I normally would only see them for a brief time, but this time they kept moving toward Sweetie and me.

They emerged from the tall grass about one hundred yards away from where I was walking. They immediately focused their collective gaze in my direction. I almost tripped as I walked, not from the bumpy terrain but from Sweetie repeatedly attempting to position her body in between my legs as I walked.

"What is wrong with you?" I asked as I almost fell on my face for a second time. I had to stop moving forward, and Sweetie pressed her body as low to the ground as she could get, her body starting to shake. It was abundantly clear that she was afraid and was staying as close to me as possible for protection.

When I looked up in the direction of Judy and her pups, they were as still as stone, staring with predator intensity directly at the shaking dog lying at my feet. There was a brief moment of stillness as we looked at each other across the wind-swept field.

Suddenly, all five of my grandad's dogs lurched forward as if they had been shot out of a cannon. Clods of dirt flew in the air as they dug their paws deep into the ground to get leverage for a burst of speed. I was astonished at how quickly it happened and how they all started in perfect unison.

I looked down to see if I needed to pick Sweetie up since she was obviously nervous about the group of dogs rapidly approaching in front of us. But she was nowhere to be found. I turned around and saw Sweetie headed across the field back toward the house as fast as her short legs could carry her. Her attempt to sprint back had triggered Judy and her litter to pursue.

As I was looking back at Sweetie running to the house, five silent blurs of brown flashed by me on both sides. I was dazed by their outright speed and slowly realized that the lead dog was going to close the gap on Sweetie before she could reach the safe confines of our house. I dropped my tackle box and began sprinting with my fishing pole in hand toward the emerging crisis in the distance.

The first dog reached Sweetie and didn't try to pounce on her, but instead it ran by her. As it ran by, it reached out with its jaws and clamped tightly onto her tail. The force of the dog blasting by Sweetie with her tail in its mouth caused her to lose her balance as her back legs were pulled past her front legs as she ran. This resulted in Sweetie falling and rolling sideways repeatedly, causing her momentum to come to a screeching halt in a tumbling cloud of dust.

The other dogs arrived and immediately began circling Sweetie at an exact distance that kept her pinned with no gaps to escape. It was a perfect moving circle that now engulfed a terrified dog pressed low to the ground, eyes looking desperately for any kind of opening that she could dart through and close the final distance to the house. No gap formed. It became increasingly clear to me. This was not a game of tag; this was a circle of death.

The next thing that happened was shocking. The four adolescent pups all shot in toward Sweetie at the same time. It was as if lightning had taken on the form of four dogs. They turned Sweetie over on her back and each dog grabbed an extremity in their powerful jaws; front right leg, back left leg, front left leg, tail and pulled outward with all their might. The sheer force of them pulling at exactly the same time caused a squeal of terror to emanate from deep inside Sweetie's lungs. She was now upside down and spread out, completely helpless and exposed, her panicked eyes looking frantically around for any hope of escape. There was none. Judy had kept circling until Sweetie had been subdued and exposed. In a flash, she bared her fangs, her shoulder muscles coiled, and she lunged in on Sweetie's exposed neck.

It's amazing what the potential of death can do to the adrenal glands. I'm pretty sure that was the fastest sprint I have ever run in my life. In no time I inserted myself into the kill zone. I wielded my fishing pole as if I were the personification of Zorro in the flesh. I was screaming and swinging my pole in a frantic motion at the five dogs, doing everything I could do to somehow get them to release their prey.

As the dust flew into the air, they suddenly released their powerful jaws that had been clamped on Sweetie's appendages. They took several steps back and started to circle again, around *me*! I said, "It's okay, Sweetie, I got this." Then I looked down at my feet and noticed she wasn't there. She had escaped during the melee and was hightailing it to the house.

I suddenly realized this was not a good situation. There was no help coming for me in the middle of the pasture. No one was home. I was on my own.

The dogs' synchronized stare on me as they circled sent a chill down my spine. Few people in the modern world are the subject of an organized pack of carnivores. Take my word for it, it is terrifying.

After a couple of circles, they suddenly broke rank and trotted off as if someone had given them a command. I stood there with my heart pumping so hard I thought it would blow a hole in my chest.

The pack headed off toward the tree line that ran along the edge of the pasture. They suddenly disappeared into the shadows of the trees.

I moved back toward the pond to retrieve my tackle box. I then headed back to my house, constantly scanning the tree line to see any movement of the brown ghosts in the darkness.

I returned safely to my house. Shaken but safe.

I was determined to find out what type of dogs had just executed a perfectly synchronized attack without any training. I had been around a lot of hunting dogs, but I had never seen anything like that. There was something special about Judy and her pups.

We lived on a dirt road in the country, and the Internet was a long way from being invented, so I needed to get to a library to find a book on dog breeds. I pleaded with my mom to take me to the library in the city. Later that week she took me with her to run some errands in the city. When I got to the public library, I wound my way to the aisle of books I was searching for and found a huge illustrated dog breed book that looked like it must contain every dog breed ever recorded. I dragged it off the shelf and carried it to a desk. I started at the front of the book, looking at each picture of the breed of dogs. It was alphabetical, so I methodically flipped through the pictures. As I flipped through each page, I became despondent. There were no pictures that resembled my granddad's dogs. I knew they had to be in there because my granddad would only buy full-blooded dogs.

I had carefully flipped through over half the alphabet, *A*s through *Q*s. Nothing. When I got to the *R*s, I flipped a page and suddenly gasped. There it was! I had to do a double take as I peered at the brown dog with the ridge of hair running the opposite way of the rest of its coat. I could've sworn it was an actual picture of Judy!

I peered intently at the title of the breed. It was a Rhodesian Ridgeback.

As I began to read about the breed, I quickly realized that this was not just another common dog breed my grandfather had brought home. There was a long history and purpose to this breed that had crossed the oceans and continents, beginning at the southern tip of Africa.

European explorers began arriving on the Cape of Good Hope in the sixteenth century. The colony continued to grow until it stretched for hundreds of miles to the north. These settlements were host to large herds of livestock belonging to the European settlers. It didn't take long for native predatorial animals to take notice of the slow-moving cattle and sheep. They were easy targets for a hungry, aggressive predator.

The fences that kept the livestock in were no match for all the African carnivores. Soon shredded livestock carcasses littered the fields. The predators doing the most damage were lions. The lions dominated the territory of Southern Africa. The prides of lions were the undisputed lords of the plains, unmatched and unchallenged by any other animal in Africa.

The settlers quickly realized they would need to go on the offensive. If they didn't, they would run out of livestock and continue to be in constant danger of being hunted, mauled, and even eaten themselves.

They began importing some of the largest and swiftest sight-hunting dogs in all of Europe. Ships started arriving at the Cape containing large numbers of Great Danes, Bullmastiffs, Greyhounds, and Salukis. Large bloodhounds were also brought in for their tenacious tracking instinct as well as their amazing ability to hunt by scent. They were renowned for their prowess in tracking deer and wild boar as well as humans.

The landowners were eager to begin hunting and eradicating the lions that were decimating their herds. With great optimism, hunts were organized, and the dogs were released to find and kill the lions.

There was only one problem.

Europe contained no predators like lions.

The big dogs did what big dogs do. They would see their prey. They would engage their prey. They would swiftly close the distance, dominate, and bring down their prey.

Simple.

However, lions aren't simple. They are ancient killing machines.

A big hunting dog has no chance against the massive claws, fangs, size, and ferocity of an African lion. The problem is that the dogs did not know that. They had never encountered one.

They were easily able to find and corner the lions. But the dogs would attack a lion one at a time. The result was painfully predictable. Before the hunters could arrive, dead and injured dogs would be littering the field. This was the case over and over. It was not working. Their dogs were helping the settlements by raising the alarm if a lion got close, which was somewhat of a deterrent. But the livestock continued to be killed and eaten. The situation was livable but not ideal.

As they were trying to solve the lion problem, the European settlers began to notice that the local Hottentot tribes used native dogs resembling a jackal for hunting. They were extremely effective in hunting small game. The dogs became popular with the Europeans. They noticed that the ones that had a characteristic ridge of hair running down their spine were a little more agile and effective, so they kept them to help develop better hunting dogs.

They immediately began crossbreeding them with Great Danes, mastiffs, greyhounds, and salukis in an attempt to somehow develop a dog that could engage the predators of Africa and win.

Little by little a new breed of dog emerged. This new breed started to fill the ranks of the settlements. The Europeans soon decided to try out their new breed in a desperate attempt to counter the lions.

During a hunt the dogs ran swiftly and silently through the rough terrain. They were almost undetectable as they sliced through the African bush. In no time they could effortlessly locate a lion. They would quickly isolate it and begin to silently circle it. They always stayed out of striking distance of the powerful swipes from the massive claw-laced paws. They were continually moving, feigning an attack from multiple directions at once, keeping the lion uncomfortable and stressed. If the lion lunged, the circle would expand and immediately contract back around the frustrated predator. The circle continued to move, offering no clear target. The ridgebacks trusted one another not to run away from the roar but to stay committed to pinning the lion down, which kept each dog protected from a focused attack. In this manner they could effectively hold a lion at bay and keep one another safe until their master arrived to take it down.

The incredible skill and bravery of this new breed to effectively hunt and corner lions earned it the name "African lion hound." Their reputation for unity and fearlessness became legendary across southern Africa. In fact, they were so aggressive at bringing down lions, they came close to eradicating the entire lion population in southern Africa. They literally had to be pulled back.

Over the years borders were drawn and nations formed in southern Africa. Many of the dogs were located in an area just north of what is currently South Africa. The country was called Rhodesia until it was later renamed Zimbabwe. During this time the breed was officially titled "Rhodesian ridgehound."

The attack I had observed in the field on the plains of Oklahoma was the result of four centuries of specialized breeding of dogs spanning the continents of Europe and Africa for the sole purpose of hunting and bringing down what is considered to this very day "the king of beasts."

The lesson I learned that day from my encounter with those African lion hounds would serve as a catalyst for the lions I would face in the future.

It was not the powerful and stately big dogs going at it alone that would bring down the lion. They didn't need to own their part since they weren't part of a pack. There was no part to own. It was the ordinary dogs working as a team and owning their individual parts that would strike fear in the heart of the lion and ultimately win the day. Their commitment not to run from the roar but to swarm with relentless intensity and devotion to one another is what made them so formidable.

Everyone is infatuated with the idea of the "big dog" that steps into any situation with confidence, talent, and a big personality that wins the day. This is no different from the belief that "the hit" is the best way to exert influence in our world. But these myths are simply not true. In the unity of the pack, powerful influence is unleashed. Ordinary ownership is an untapped force that can infuse life into a movement.

Having the correct mentality is crucial to create ownership with volunteers and employees. Most organizations operate with a big-dog mentality. They are obsessed with identifying the most talented leaders and training them at a high level to increase their capacity to lead. A plan and a desire to raise up leaders are essential to any successful organization, but it

> **Ordinary ownership is an untapped force that can infuse life into a movement.**

needs to be done with a simultaneous commitment and value of the ordinary. This is accomplished with a pack mentality that seeks to create the conditions that unleash the influence of ownership. When your volunteers or employees understand and aggressively own their part in your organization, a pack will form that will hunt and bring down any lions the big dogs can't conquer on their own.

Do your volunteers own their part to the point of standing their ground with their teammates in the face of adversity, or are they simply waiting for the big dogs to take on the lions your organization is facing? The answer could be the difference between constantly engaging lions and actually bringing them down.

RECAP

Don't run from risk by lowering the bar of expectation for volunteers. Raising the bar can reveal the heroes that are otherwise unseen.

Our culture and our organizations are infatuated with being the big dog. Many times the only way to bring down the lions you face is a pack of ordinary dogs. Pursue ownership and release the pack.

Final Thoughts

The Andes

The Andean Mountains are the longest continental mountain range in the world. High in the Andes of Peru, at certain times of the day, when the wind dies down and the clouds separate just enough to let the sunlight briefly through, you can look closely on top of a frozen boulder and detect a slight movement under the ice. It is a small trickle of water that moves slowly down the rock as the sun warms the surface.

That trickle meanders down small cracks and crevices in the rocky outcrops and ground until another trickle of water connects with it creating a slight increase in downward momentum. These trickles spread and connect with other trickles forming a small stream. That stream slowly meanders down the steep mountain to eventually intersect with other streams. This interconnected multiplication of streams catalyzes into a river which swells with each additional stream and tributary. The maze of momentum becomes more centralized until four thousand miles later the

Amazon River smashes into the Atlantic Ocean with the force of 685,695 cubic inches per second, causing the salty ocean to become fresh water for thirty miles.

Every movement starts as a trickle. Every trickle is a person. If the conditions are just right, that person, just like the slight trickle of warm water on a frozen surface, will naturally move in a direction. The path may be undetermined and flow through crags and crevices, but there will be movement. Soon that person will connect with other individuals who are similar. They aren't contained by the frozen environment around them. They are equally warm and moving as well. A natural connection creates more momentum. Their synchronized direction leads to further run-ins with other people flowing the same direction. The strength of the flow is palpable and visible. Suddenly they are part of a river of people flowing the same direction with stunning power. They are *influere*, flowing into the valley. They are influence. They are a movement.

Welcome to the top of the Andes!

We have gone on a journey together examining some principles that help create trickles of movement in volunteers. We have looked at the incredible importance of creating and bestowing value on your volunteers. We amplified the need to strive for being simple and concise in what we are asking our volunteers to accomplish. We also examined what happens when we identify a common enemy, which unlocks powerful unity. Finally, we have taken a brief look at what it looks like when volunteers passionately own their part in your organization.

I continue to learn more about these principles. Movements are made up of people. Those people and circumstances constantly change and can be highly unpredictable. Anyone who claims to have figured out the one formula that can create and sustain a movement of the masses is not being honest. But I do know that conditions can be created to help cultivate and spark movements with volunteers, and I will continue attempting to create those conditions until my last breath is allowed on this earth.

I wonder what new movements are currently waiting out there for you to discover. You may consider yourself to be just a small trickle in this world compared to the vast ocean of life. Congratulations! You are perfectly gifted and positioned to join others and exert influence on those around you as you flow into your world today. You never know where your movement will take you.